Government Institutes Internet Series

Emergency Planning

on the INTERNET

Rick Tobin
Ryan Tobin

Government Institutes, Inc.
Rockville, Maryland

Government Institutes, Inc., 4 Research Place, Rockville, Maryland 20850, USA.

01   00   99   98   97   5   4   3   2   1

Library of Congress Cataloging-in-Publication Data

Tobin, Patrick D.
       Emergency planning and management on the internet / by Patrick D. Tobin, Ryan P. Tobin.
               p.   cm.
       Includes bibliographical references and index.
       ISBN: 0-86587-600-2
       1. Emergency management--Computer network resources. 2. Internet (computer network).   I. Tobin, Ryan P. II. Title
    HV551.2.T63   1997
    025.06'658477--dc21
                                                      97-44667
                                                      CIP

Printed in the United States of America

This book is dedicated to the memory of Doyle Workman, California Governor's Office of Emergency Services: a talented member of the emergency management community, a trusted colleague, and a wonderful, caring person. He will be missed.

Table of Contents

Foreword

You hear your associates bragging about the Internet everyday, as if it were some magic potion. You may have wondered how to put the Internet to use for your work in disaster management. And if you are a member of the public, outside the emergency management ranks, you were probably puzzled and confused by all the terminology and organizations surrounding disasters.

This book was written for the professional disaster manager because no such single source existed to lead to the wealth and variety of information on the Internet. It was also written so that the public, who pays for emergency management services, can investigate the essential work being done, and perhaps become a stronger supporter of emergency management programs.

There are many books on other aspects of the Internet, including how to gather information from it, but none provide the disaster focus. And you are just in time! By reading this book, and using the techniques it provides, you will be entering a realm that is growing exponentially. Some sources estimate that over ten thousand Web Sites on the Internet focus on disaster information. And these ten thousand lead to thousands of others. Without this handy reference you truly could be lost in cyberspace, like a dizzy frog in a whirlpool.

As someone who was sitting right where you are, not long ago, I can only say, "Hold on!" When you find out what you have missed you will be stunned. You will also be thrilled to have found a new tool for life.

Rick Tobin
President, TAO Services
Emergency Management Consultants
El Dorado, California

Preface

For the last three years I've shared the frustration of many line staff in emergency management organizations. Some managers and computer information specialists are still not convinced of the value of the Internet as a daily tool for every professional involved in disaster preparedness. This puzzles me and many others who do the daily work before, during and after disasters. Emergency management staff, who could not wait to have access, got on line privately and were shocked to find what valuable resources had been prohibited at work. Here were volumes of information on every subject we struggled with from day to day. Here was instant access to regulations and laws that took days of work to research, sometimes without success. And, there was instant contact with other professionals—other minds who could give immediate feedback from their experience.

To help convince those who controlled the use of computers and staff resources that there was value in the Internet, I began distributing a spreadsheet titled "Tobin Surfs the Net." It received positive response, but it was clear that without a guide to help the reader, the information remained cold and lifeless. The contents of this book were produced after months of experience in helping emergency management professionals to access the wonders of the Internet World Wide Web.

The resource you are about to explore is powerful. Some say it is the most powerful single tool since humans put pen to paper. Whether that is true or not, there is no doubt that the access to emergency management information is fabulous. The reduction of work time spent in fruitless research is incredible. The community that is being developed world wide among emergency management professionals, through e-mail, newsgroups and chat areas, is wonderful. As they said at the end of *Casablanca*, "This could be the beginning of a beautiful relationship."

About the Authors

As owner of TAO Services for 10 years, Rick Tobin has provided emergency planning consultation for local, state, and federal agencies, as well as small business and industry. His experience covers the gamut of emergency planning, including natural and technological disasters. Mr. Tobin's specialties include the development of plans and procedures, facilities, training, and drills/exercises. Mr. Tobin has been involved in the integration of emergency management and computer technologies since 1983.

Much of Mr. Tobin's emergency management expertise comes from practical field experiences including —

- Ambulance service;
- County Disaster Council membership;
- Search-and-Rescue Team operations; and as a
- Emergency Response Team member at a copper mine, a U.S. Naval shipyard, and a civilian nuclear power plant.

Rick Tobin is also the founder of the Mass Relocation Project, a program dedicated to development and training associated with low-cost, sustainable mass care and shelter facilities for large population movements following catastrophes.

Ryan Tobin founded a large, independent public bulletin board service in 1993. He also started his own computer firm, California Coastal Computers, in 1994. His expertise has been featured in the *Sacramento Bee* and on cable television. Ryan has been teaching others how to install and use the Internet for over four years.

If you have any questions about this book, please contact the authors at rtobin@foothill.net.

Acknowledgments

I am deeply grateful to the many supportive people who helped make this book both accurate and interesting. First, and foremost, my heartfelt thanks and gratitude to my wife, Cinda, who put up with my months of struggle and worry over the text. Her ideas and corrections were invaluable.

The kind words of Avagene Moore and Art Botterell were there when I needed them. I must also thank my contacts at the California Governor's Office of Emergency Services, especially Adam Sutkus and David Zocchetti. Next, to the staff at the Natural Hazards Research Institute in Boulder Colorado, the *Stonefly Newsletter*, and the *Disaster Recovery Journal*. I must also thank my dear artist friend, John Hancock, for his incredible artwork for the front cover, which truly sets the tone for the text.

I must praise the staff of the publisher, Government Institutes, for having the vision to bring this information to both the emergency management community and the public. They suffered with me through the challenges to complete the work, especially during some personally trying times. Charlene Ikonomou, my publishing guide and mentor, was particularly gentle with her edits. Ryan and I thank you all.

I also need to give special acknowledgment to the fine people at Media Graphics International, Inc., who graciously allowed the use of their artwork for this text throughout the book. Their wonderful products have made TAO Services reports, presentations, pamphlets and Web Site come to life. We cannot say enough about the quality of their clip art and graphic media. If you are interested in their hiqh-quality products please contact them at:

Media Graphics International, Inc.
8175-A Sheridan Boulevard, Suite #355
Arvada, Colorado 80003
303-427-8808
www.media-graphics.net

1
So Much Information, So Little Time

A Brave New Tool

 How can emergency planners keep up with the constant barrage of information that comes across their desks every day? Paperwork seems to eat up the hours. What happened to the paperless office? What about keeping up with the latest information? Decades ago it was called gathering intelligence, but now it is a constant battle to sort and make meaning out of the glut of data. What one tool can make a tremendous difference in finding and sorting out the "good stuff?" The answer is the Internet, if used properly. Some still believe that the Internet will only compound the problem, especially for data junkies. This chapter will introduce you to this wonderful tool and show you what it can do for you.

Every emergency management agency has had serious reductions in funding in the last ten years. There are a few notable exceptions, but in most cases the "do more with less" mentality has nearly crippled the emergency management profession. Travel budgets have been eliminated. When was the last time you went to an out-of-state seminar or conference? Training is rare and sporadic. Trade publication subscriptions have been cut. Without personal contacts through networking it is impossible to find out what is really happening "out there," where there are other successful programs. And the future looks bleak for improving these conditions. So, what can the emergency planner do to keep current with key events and research?

Emergency planning professionals are practical people—people who find ways to serve the public and promote safety. Experience has also taught them caution. Many have encountered the vendor, or agency, who exaggerated the merits of a new program, only to be disappointed. That may be why the Internet was slow to become a tool for emergency management. But like a favorite wrench or screwdriver, the Internet will never be put aside by emergency planners once they discover how well it works for almost every project.

And what about emergency planning projects? They are innumerable! I know of few subject areas that touch almost all walks of life, every profession, and every interest group. Emergency planners must work with all levels of the public and private sector. Where is a tool that can encompass that kind of scope? Again, the Internet. It has it all. But before investigating this brave new tool, there are some basic assumptions in this text that you should understand.

Assumptions

This text was designed for people who already know some of the basics, and who may have some exposure to the Internet, perhaps by using electronic mail, known as *e-mail*. There are many trade publications and references about the Internet and how to use it, its history, structure, and purpose. Some of these resources are listed in Appendix D, References. A very helpful text, if you are a novice, is "Safety and Health on the Internet," by Ralph B. Stuart.

Ryan and Rick Tobin have strong biases about hardware and the use of computers. Emergency management is very businesslike, and business people use IBM™ compatible equipment. The authors also feel that Microsoft™ provides some of the best software for computer applications, but not for the personal computer (*pc*). The authors' bias is to use Netscape Navigator™ on a IBM PC. If you use other systems (such as a MacIntosh) or other software (such as Internet Explorer™) you can still use the information in this text, but you may need to adapt it to your system configuration.

The authors have also assumed that the reader has access to the Internet and an Internet Service Provider (*ISP*). The reader should also have access to assistance from an Information Management specialist for questions about access and connections to the Internet. If you have not made a strong connection to these folks in your organization, make it your first task.

This book will not make you an expert on the Internet. However, it will help you utilize the World Wide Web section of the Internet to improve and expand your ability to perform emergency planning. There are a lot of steps to becoming proficient at using the Internet; this book is just the first one.

Finally, this book is designed to be fun, because the Internet is fun. If you follow the guidance in this book, and the books recommended to support it, you will make fewer mistakes. *But you will make mistakes.* And that is okay. That is how people learn. You will be surprised after just two or three sessions on the Internet. Any bumps along the way will seem minor. It is like riding a bicycle. Did you refuse to learn because you thought you might fall? No. Did you refuse to take on emergency management because it was complex? No. So it is with the Internet. Just go slowly.

So What Is the Internet?

What are the absolute basics you need to know about the Internet? In its simplest form, it is no more than many computers (*servers*) with many pieces of information (*files*) hooked together for people to use (*client*). The original university and government servers have expanded exponentially each year. Privately owned servers are also now part the system; they provide Internet access for a fee. These are known as Internet Service Providers (*ISP*). They have a specific way to communicate to each other (*protocol*) over telephone lines, and in some cases by satellite. The Internet uses devices called modems to translate the language to and from your computer to the Internet servers. This system was developed to resist damage to communications caused by nuclear war. Taxes paid for its initial establishment. There are hundreds of millions of people who have used or have access to the Internet. And you will soon have access to many of them, as they will have access to you. Those are the basics.

How It Grabbed Me

When I first heard about the Internet in the late 1980s, I was very curious about what this communications tool was all about. I had used modems in the 1970s to transmit data back and forth across the country while working in a Shell Research Laboratory, outside of Houston, Texas. It was clear then that this technology had some incredible possibilities. But it was not until I started getting serious enough to take classes about the Internet in 1990s that I begin to see what was coming. And it was huge! There were already serious needs for Internet support in the emergency planning areas I worked in, but only a few computer maniacs seemed to understand what the Internet was and how to use it.

Early on, I was amazed at the Internet's ability to hunt for information through such early search engines as Gopher and Veronica. But those searches still required some special language, computer semantics skills, and lots of time. The breakthrough came with the development of the World Wide Web (*WWW* or *Web*), which pushed its way to the top of Internet use. Regardless of what you have heard, the Web is not all of the Internet, by any means. But it is where the most exciting things are happening in emergency management.

Then came the rush of the advanced search engines and the wonderful graphical browsers like Netscape™ and platforms like Yahoo™. These softwares enable millions of users to access incredible amounts of information directly from sources around the globe, day or night. Users who needed pictures and sound now have the ability to find things in a friendlier environment.

Some computer purists will tell you that not knowing every detail about how the software interacts leaves you somewhat illiterate. Our response is, emergency planners do not have time to become computer experts. Software design changes like the wind. Planners just want to use a tool. They do not want the entire story about how it was manufactured, how it was designed, and how it was shipped. There are lots of problem nails out there for emergency planners to hammer down. Just point out the hammers so the planners can get the job done!

When I Knew It Was True

In 1995 I began exploring the Internet seriously. There were a few places that had access, like the public library, where I could surf a bit at a reasonable cost. At that time my rural location did not have local ISPs. So, as a wonderful gift to dear old Dad, my son Ryan bought a six month Internet access subscription to one of the first local ISPs. He set up my computer and voilà. It was love at first byte!

Within an hour I found topics and information I would never have found in a library. Within a month I was surfing hard, and beginning to find more and more small references to emergency management sites. By the summer of 1996 I began to see that every emergency professional, not just the planners, needed to have access everyday. But it was impossible to find a concise, organized emergency management site directory.

So, I developed "Tobin Surfs the Net," a spread sheet of emergency management Web sites that could be easily sorted and scanned by subject and content. I worked on it for months on my own time, hoping to convince my own state agency to open up Internet access to staff, and not just to upper management.

To be blunt, my project was ignored. A few people took off with it and got excited, but management still slammed the door on the "worker bee" access. This was happening all over the U.S.. I got calls from emergency planners in other states asking for the "Tobin Surfs the Net." We were all trying to get management to listen...but management was not interested. It was going to take a disaster or two to get their attention.

And then it happened—the floods of Winter 96-97. I do not mean just in California. I mean all over the U.S.. The Internet use for emergency management started hopping. It was used heavily in California for such things as weather forecasts, river gauge tracking, agency updates, e-mail, mapping and incredible amounts of other data sharing. There was no doubt that there would never be another major disaster in the U.S. that would not feature, heavily, the use of the Internet. I was there. I used it in the floods. Everyone was hooked. My spreadsheet of emergency management sites was invaluable. Management changed their minds.

Now, line staff in many emergency management organizations are getting direct access to the World Wide Web and e-mail. It is a new world for emergency management and the Internet. You can be part of it.

Bright Ideas: Take your Information Management Specialist to lunch today. Ask them if they can help you get:

✓ some assistance,

✓ updated software; and

✓ faster hardware.

2
Tools of Choice

Treasure Hunting

Treasure hunting. Your journey is about to begin. But, before you rush out into the desert you must be properly equipped. Having spent some time looking for lost gold in New Mexico myself, I can attest to what happens when you rush into the wilderness without proper provisions. I learned long ago that you should first listen to people who have been there themselves and find out what kinds of tools to take with you. Without the right equipment, you may not be able to reach the treasure, or even recognize it when you find it. Much worse is the possibility of making the trip so miserable that finding the treasure will be minor compared to survival and returning in one piece. So, before you start that expedition, use this chapter to outfit yourself to head into the unknown.

NOTE: One of the assumptions of the authors is that readers already know some of the basics about the operation of a computer and the basic terminology of the parts. If you are not ready, please consider one of the texts found under the appendix entitled References.

The Buying Frenzy

The struggle to purchase and stay current with the latest technology can be daunting. The day that the new computer is first sitting on the desktop is the day it has already become outmoded. It is impossible to ensure that it is not only the fastest machine you can afford, but the most reasonably priced. For example, at the time of this writing, there is a portable 486 laptop sitting next to the desk in the office that cost over $3000 in 1994. That same laptop could be purchased in 1997 for less than $1000. (Psychologists call this cognitive dissonance.) It can drive you to distraction, so just ignore it. Accept the fact that for whatever computer you purchase the quality will improve and the price will drop. Just get the best quality you can at the time you buy equipment, and make sure the unit can be upgraded as new improvements are developed.

The Need for Speed

There are two basic needs for comfortably exploring and using the Internet: speed and storage capacity. It is frustrating to wait for graphics to load, to be unable to download large files quickly, and to transmit large e-mails that tie up the rest of the computer. And, when a treasure trove of information is discovered, it is maddening not to be able to store it safely away just because there is not enough storage capacity.

Some computer aficionados will say that when it comes to speed and computing, too fast is not fast enough. Emergency planners have similar compulsions. There is just too much to do in a day. A computer should provide instant information. The PC is not supposed to be the slowest link in the process of gathering data, yet often it is for several reasons. Budget is the main reason. It is hard to imagine how many jurisdictions are so financially strapped that staff are still using Apple II computers, or 286 clones inherited from the accounting department. If you find yourself in this situation, have hope. There are some ways to come up to the new technologies. You shouldn't feel any more deprived than the emergency planners who were tricked into buying 386 machines just before the 486 emerged. Remember the old joke, "What's the difference between a used car salesman and a computer salesman? Answer: The used car salesman knows when he's lying."

So what do you look for to ensure you have the speed you need? First, megahertz (**MHz**), the baseline speed of data transmission within the computer. This is changing so fast that within a year of printing of this book, the speeds noted here will be archaic. But in 1997 speeds, the target for your best tool is a computer that can provide 200 MHz of computing speed. That is bound to be a standard consideration for most emergency planning work until the year 2000. And with this speed consider no less than 32 megabytes of Random Access Memory (**RAM**). Why? Because the RAM means capacity to do multi-tasking. When the Internet is on the screen you can manipulate the data quickly in several programs. With the visual and sound elements becoming prevalent components of the Internet environment, poor RAM availability will mean increasing frustration. Luckily, the price of additional RAM, however, is dropping.

Memory—the Place for Stuff

George Carlin is right when he says we just go around life collecting a lot of "stuff." Emergency planners are famous for being packrats of information, reports, documents, guides, and regulations that might someday be important for some critical budget analysis, a policy paper, a new procedure and occasionally an actual emergency response. Face it, you need space to save all that "stuff." So do not go cheap on hard drive space. You can never have too much space, especially with all the huge databases you will want to load and the picture of disaster sites, the Geographic Information System (**GIS**) files, and the background sounds for presentations. Hard drive space is becoming not only cheaper but more condensed. There are megabyte disks you can carry in your pocket--the information that an entire PC could hold just a few years ago. If the predictions of the hardware developers are correct, many PCs will have compact disc (**CD**) writing capability as a standard component by the year 2000. Simply get as much storage space as possible. You'll need it all.

Modems

Imagine the search for gold takes you into a land where you must have a translator. Are you going to go cheap and get one that "kinda-sorta" knows the language of the natives? I think not. You will want the best you can find: one that is efficient, clearly communicates with few mistakes, and gets the message right the first time. The same rule works for modems.

Buying a cheap modem is like putting the wrong gasoline in your 4x4. You need that vehicle for exploration. Why gum up the works? Do you really want performance? Here's where to get it. Buy the fastest, most reliable modem on the market. There will be lots of contenders, and you may have to decide whether to go with an internal or external model. Still, read the specifications carefully. The authors are very biased and recommend U.S. Robotics products because of their quality, reliability, and value for cost. They are also one of the world's leaders and will be in business next week, whereas others may not. At the time of this writing, the 56 kbs modems are hitting the streets for general consumption. If you can get one at that speed, do so. If you can't, settle for nothing less than a 28.8 kbs device. Anything less will bog you down and leave you high and dry, tying up your machine and eating up expensive access costs. Time is money, and time is based on speed.

To Fax or Not to Fax

The authors also recommend that you ensure your set up includes faxing capacity through your modem. This will become an essential part of your data management and information management for emergency planning operations. Do not depend on that clunky fax machine back in the office.

Cable Modems

Cable modems are just arriving on the marketplace. If they are available in your community, take full advantage of this incredible upgrade. Your surfing can be a breeze at speeds in the range of 400 kbs, depending on the capabilities of your cable provider. Until you've seen the demonstrations, you have no idea what kind of power this brings to your office. In emergency response, the ability of your emergency operations center to receive, process, analyze, and transmit data over the Internet can be increased ten fold. The authors recommend this technology.

Monitors

While the physical size of computers and memory storage shrinks, monitors keep getting larger. And they should since baby boomers are now in their era of bifocals. People want brighter, faster, clearer screens even on their palm top PCs. Size is important, no doubt. But when you buy a monitor, look for quality and reliability. Your monitor will probably last beyond several computers and many upgrades. The authors recommend nothing less than super VGA, 17 inch with .28 dot pitch, capable of at least 1024x768 resolution. Digital (button) controls are preferable over analog (dials and knobs). If you can get a larger screen, buy it.

Other Hardware

Video Cards

Video card prices have plummeted. The quality of video cards is getting better every year. There is a lot of competition in this field. Make sure the card you choose is robust enough to handle television quality transmissions. This will become necessary as more capabilities for clear video transmission are available in the very near future. Remember that the World Wide Web is a graphical environment. A fast, high-end video card can add luster to your experience on the Internet. The authors' recommendation is to use at least 2 megabytes of VRAM, if not 4. Some good companies are Number Nine, ATI, Matrox, and Diamond. Also, many video cards now have 3D acceleration of some sort. Make sure to get that option if it is available. The video card is one of the key reasons you will need more RAM to boost everything from graphics interfaces to deep views of GIS files.

Sound Cards

The authors have used the Internet for both voice and video transmission. A sound card is critical for the audio section, and many sites now feature video clips with information emergency planners can use later in presentations, or for transfer to video tape. The authors recommend Creative Labs Sound Blaster products, 16-bit at a minimum. The AWE32 is a big step up from 16-bit sound, and should be considered a good investment in sound quality. Of course, you'll need quality speakers to ensure your Internet sound experience is also of value.

CD ROM

CD ROM technology is moving faster than the needs of consumers. You don't need mega-speed CD power to surf the net, but you may need it to take advantage of some of the useful Internet products that are now on CD, including reference banks of Internet sites. This can save time and hard drive space. The authors recommend at least quad speed, but you are probably going to use six or eight speed models. NEC, Sony, Plextor, and Teac are fairly common and reliable.

Printers

Printer quality is also changing dramatically. By the year 2000, the use of color laser printers will be the standard in most offices. Color lasers are still expensive for most emergency planner uses, but if you produce exercise manuals, develop maps, and write procedures it may be worth the investment. There are some laser printers on the market now that produce a 600 dpi color print on regular paper in the $4000-7000 price range. That price tag is bound to drop significantly. To use the Internet for your maximum benefit, you should have the best laser printer you can purchase, with a minimum of 600 dpi printing. The graphics on the Internet are improving as well and your use of those graphics can make a huge difference in your documents.

Scanners

The use of reasonably priced scanners is of questionable value for most emergency planning purposes. Anything you want to capture and bring into the Internet, e.g. onto your home page, should only be done on very high quality graphical scanners. The average daily use of a scanner doesn't justify buying one for Internet work in emergency planning. It is far cheaper to have your Information Management specialist handle the scanning details.

Providers

You may have very little choice in selecting your Internet Service Provider. Most organizations leave those decisions to the Information Management staff. If you do, however, have the power to decide there are several items to consider:

✓ **Why**: You need a provider as a doorway to the Internet.

✓ **Who**: You will have a selection from national services like America Online, your local phone companies, national phone services, cable companies, and independent smaller suppliers. Be prepared to shift over to a back-up provider in case the primary fails.

✓ **Where**: There are qualified local companies who will also offer you their wares and it will only cost you their fee plus a local phone call. If you must travel widely you may want to use an ISP that provides national support.

✓ **When**:   Ensure that the service is available 24-hours-a-day. Also ensure that the ISP has a policy of informing its clients if the service will be down for maintenance, or if it is off line due to a technical problem. If the service will not make this promise you could be caught short if a disaster response required access.

✓ **How**:   Decide on the value of a monthly or annual contract. A monthly contract allows evaluation of the ISP and you can drop the service if it does not meet your needs. A yearly contract may be cheaper, however, and will allow for some amenities at no extra charge.

✓ **What**:   Ensure that your service provides you, at a minimum, e-mail services and full Internet access. Ask if they provide Web site space and assistance in placing a Web Site. Determine if there are size limits for your Web Site. Find out if the ISP provides installation software for the Internet (they usually do) and if they provide customer support. You also want to know how many lines the ISP can handle conveniently, since during heavy use times the EOC will need assured access. Also ensure that the ISP can support the speed of line service you require. If the ISP cannot support 56 kbs modems then the hardware upgrade will be of little benefit.

✓ **Cost**:   A flat fee is usually best. Do not look at a low base rate and think it is cheaper. Your Internet hours will add up fast. It is better to purchase an unlimited rate. Also find out what the charges are for additional line connections at the same site. If your entire EOC is tied to the Internet it could be a substantial cost over having one or two stations with access.

Software

There are several software tools you will need for effective Internet access. First, a standard PC-based DOS platform. The authors lean towards Windows™, and

Windows 95™. Purchase the most recent version available. Windows NT™ is becoming the standard for most offices with any type of networking capability.

Second, you will need to choose from one of a myriad of softwares that work from the PC-based DOS platform to reach your ISP. The authors recommend Trumpet Winsock™ for the Windows 3.1™ class of environments, but your ISP may provide another. Windows 95™ needs no additional software for standard Internet use, whether via modem or LAN.

Third, you will need an Internet browser. As stated earlier, the authors recommend Netscape Navigator™ for Internet browsing software. Others, like Microsoft Explorer™, also work well.

You will also need software for electronic mail (e-mail). There are dozens available, and they all offer at least the basics. The authors recommend Eudora Pro™.

Other capabilities can be utilized with your browser, such as Java™. The authors do not recommend you use the Java™ capacity in your browser for security reasons. Other applications, known as plug-ins, may also be added to the browsers capacity. These can be loaded directly from a site that requires their use to take full advantage of the formats and tools used at that particular site.

Phone Line Services

There are some incredible new hardware adaptations that can be added to your standard, two-wire wrapped copper phone line. These will be discussed in Chapter 10. You should discuss what upgrades are available from your phone service that enhance the speed and volume of your system. Your agency may also already have Integrated Services Digital Network (ISDN) or a high volume T-1 line. Be sure to investigate what types of lines are available as this can have substantial impact on the quality of your Internet use.

Security and Virus Protection

There is always some danger involved with any expedition. Be sure to take matches to keep away any lurking beast. It is also wise to be inoculated before stepping into a disease infested jungle. So, before you venture forth blindly, meet with an Information Management specialist. Find out the latest information about setting up firewalls and other security devices you may need to protect your side of the fence when you go to the Internet, and to protect your Web Site. Make sure the specialist has some method of periodically running a virus checker on your system. The latest versions are also available over the Internet. The authors recommend, for general purposes, Norton Antivirus™. The specialist should also warn you about what files you should or should not load from the Internet.

For managers who want to limit staff usage, there are a number of software solutions your Information Management specialist can suggest. In reality, abuses by employees are far less problematic than commonly believed. Millions of employees successfully and respectfully use the Internet each day for their work, including emergency planners.

Costs

With the cuts in funding for almost all emergency planning programs it may seem a daunting act to justify these costs, or even find a source to pay for the correct tools. But there are options. Unfortunately, one of the best is to have a major federal disaster in your area. Once the formal declaration occurs, dollars may be available to upgrade your response capability, and that includes all of the tools for the Internet. It will not pay for continuing costs of the ISP or the phone lines, but the basic units can be covered.

Another great source (outside of your general fund) is from other fee sources charged by your agency for related functions. For instance, it is not a leap to justify that some of the hazardous material operations impact emergency planning. Local administrators have shown this value in the past based on the close ties with hazardous materials response and emergency planning. The same can be said for some special fire and law funding.

One example of special law enforcement funding that may assist you is the increasing workload and support for terrorism planning. Look carefully at all funding sources coming from these federal programs to see how much of your Internet access needs can be supported. As you will see later, the Internet has a plethora of data and current information on terrorism and emergency planning.

Another source, for interim needs, is the hand-me-down. But get leftovers from a department that is always ahead of everyone else. Their second bests may be equal to or better than the minimums you need. This is where the lunches with the Information Management specialist are so valuable. Ask the specialist if someone is going to be upgrading soon and then try to get access to the best leftovers.

Finally, there is always the vendor route. Many manufacturers are sympathetic to emergency planner needs, and if their factory or outlet is in the community, they benefit by a more effective emergency response and recovery. It never hurts to ask if you can show them your needs and where the shortfalls are, along with justification for the tools you need to be more effective. They might even help sponsor your Web Site at their cost if you leave their logo or a bit of credit in the Web page.

Minimums

But what are the minimums? The reader may have older equipment. What is the baseline for equipment and software that an emergency planner should have to just start the process of using the Internet? The authors believe a minimum set up for success will require the following, if the reader cannot afford newer equipment:

HARDWARE
486 66 MHz CPU
1 Gigabyte hard drive
16 megabytes of RAM
SVGA 1 megabyte video card
28.8 kbs modem
Standard phone line and jack

SOFTWARE
Windows 3.x™
Trumpet Winsock™ (or comparable ISP access software)
Netscape Navigator™ (or comparable browser)
Eudora Pro™ (or comparable e-mail software)

Basic Research Tools

There are a few basic tools you should bring to the table before you begin your search for the buried treasures in the Internet:

✓ Know what you are looking for, and be specific. If you look for broad areas, you could waste huge amounts of time. The lists provided later in this text will help you narrow your searches before you even boot up the computer.

✓ Do not expect to find everything on the Internet. There is an incredible amount of information on the Internet. However, a good public library is still the source for complete data you may never find on the World Wide Web or any other locations on the Internet. Do not let the Internet become your only source of information.

✓ Verify information from the Internet. Don't take everything on the Internet at face value. Ensure that the agency or organization posting the information is responsible. You may be at risk if you use their data without due diligence.

✓ Remember that the information on the Internet is usually copyrighted by the people who own the Web sites. Be careful how you use the posted information. If you need to use the material verbatim in another document to be published, be sure to get permission from the original author (who may not be the same person as the person who owns the Web site).

✓ Set time limits for yourself every time you venture into the Internet. This ensures you will stay focused in your search and prevent you from drifting around aimlessly.

✓ When visiting a site, make a quick assessment of what a site offers. It may be outdated information, or incomplete, but the site could have a bookmark to another site that would be invaluable.

Training

Probably the most important tool of all is your state of preparedness. There are many ways to acquire training other than by reading this text. Seminars can be of tremendous assistance for providing a solid base prior to your total commitment to the Internet experience. Universities, colleges, and local educational networks are also an excellent source of training. The authors also recommend that parents visit their children's school and ask the computer instructors there for information. In addition, there are many computer users groups across the country that will be glad to assist you as you learn about this brave new tool.

Bright Ideas:

Take your Internet Service Provider to lunch today. Ask the specialist to help you with:

✓ some ideas about speed/quality hardware upgrades,

✓ updated software for Internet access and use; and space for your Internet Web site and support to construct it.

3
Internet Emergency Web Sites

A Manager's Viewpoint

Some management specialists want step-by-step guidance for using the Internet for emergency management. Some, however, have the philosophy of, "Eat your dessert first, life is short." They prefer Web Sites to be listed first. They'll look at the other chapters when they need them. To meets the needs of this second group, we put the entire listing at the beginning of the book. If you are one of the professionals in this field who just wants the surface ore, here it is. However, for those of you who want the deeper treasures, please dig into Chapters 4-10. It will be worth the effort.

The listings have been grouped by topic and use, from the experience of a seasoned emergency management professional. This approach should be useful and dynamic for almost any contingency. Some of the sites present topics that might not be considered relevant to emergency management, but these sites are critical tools that can enhance your efficiency at performing your day-to-day tasks (e.g., the online thesaurus, phone directories, maps, etc.).

A detailed description of how to use the listing is provided in Chapter 4. As you read through this list remember two critical points: 1) the sites listed will lead to many other sites that are not present here and, 2) the list URL addresses may change. If a URL reference returns with an error message during your searches, you may have to use the tools and techniques described in Chapter 6 to find the new location for that Web Site.

The opinions about the content and design of the Web Sites are strictly those of the authors, and do not reflect the interests or bias of any organization or corporation, including Government Institutes.

Topics in the Web Site List

The following topic areas listed below have Web Sites on the following pages. This list is provided as a quick reference for the reader, depending on the specific area of interest.

- Animals
- Asteroids/Comets
- Avalanche
- Business Recovery
- Climate
- Communications
- Computer Recovery
- Earthquake
- Emergency Alert System
- Emergency Management
- Emergency Supplies
- Environment
- Fire
- Flood
- General Topics
- Geology

- Government
- Hazardous Materials
- Health/Medical
- Hurricane
- Insurance
- Landslide
- Law Enforcement
- Laws/Regulations
- Lightning
- Maps
- Mitigation
- Mutual Aid
- Nuclear
- Preparedness
- Recovery
- Relief

- Research
- Risk Management
- Satellite Information
- Search & Rescue
- Space Science
- Stress
- Terrorism
- Tools
- Tornado
- Training
- Transportation
- Tsunami
- Vendors
- Volcano
- Volunteers
- Weather

The List

ANIMALS

Pets and Disasters Fact Sheets			
Federal Emergency Management Agency (FEMA)			
http://www.fema.gov/fema/petsf.html			
GRAPHICS	LINKS	NEWSLETTER	LAWS/REGS

Includes:
- Before Disaster
- During Disaster
- After Disaster

A brief, solid guideline that can be inserted into most local response plans.

ASTEROIDS/COMETS

Asteroid and Comet Impact Analysis			
NASA's Ames Research Center			
http://ccf.arc.nasa.gov/sst/			
GRAPHICS	LINKS	NEWSLETTER	LAWS/REGS
◆	◆		

Includes:
- Overview
- Latest Updates
- Testimony and Reports
- Listing of Near Earth Objects
- Further Reading
- Images and Animation
- Related Web Sites and Pages

Interesting, but you hope you never have to use this data. Everything for the big one.

AVALANCHE

Colorado Avalanche Information Center (CAIC)			
Colorado Geological Survey			
http://www.netway.net/caic			
GRAPHICS	LINKS	NEWSLETTER	LAWS/REGS
◆	◆		

Includes:
- Avalanche Histories and Summaries
- Mountain Weather and Avalanche Reports
- Warnings
- Hotline Numbers
- Avalanche Education
- Books and Videos
- Links to Related Sites

Avalanche forecasting and education. For managers planning in mountain regions.

BUSINESS RECOVERY

Disaster Recovery Journal Home Page, for contingency planning			
Disaster Recovery Journal			
http://www.drj.com			
GRAPHICS	LINKS	NEWSLETTER	LAWS/REGS
	◆	◆	

Includes:
- Conferences
- On-line Magazine
- Article Archive
- Vendor Directory
- Daily News Briefs

A great site with a focus on business sector emergency management in all subject areas. Lots of information, but password required to get to some valuable articles. Excellent links. Has a chat area. Provides job opportunity listings.

BUSINESS RECOVERY

<table>
<tr><td colspan="4">Emergency Management Guide for Business and Industry
Federal Emergency Management Agency (FEMA)
http://www.fema.gov/fema/bizindex.html</td></tr>
<tr><td>GRAPHICS</td><td>LINKS</td><td>NEWSLETTER</td><td>LAWS/REGS</td></tr>
<tr><td></td><td></td><td></td><td></td></tr>
<tr><td colspan="2">Includes:
• Table of Contents
• Appendix</td><td colspan="2">• Search Engine
• Feedback</td></tr>
<tr><td colspan="4"></td></tr>
<tr><td colspan="4">Everyone involved with disaster planning for business needs this site. It reflects the contents of the FEMA/ARC Guide for Business Disaster Recovery.</td></tr>
</table>

<table>
<tr><td colspan="4">Contingency Planning and Disaster Recovery
RiskINFO
http://www.disasterplan.com</td></tr>
<tr><td>GRAPHICS</td><td>LINKS</td><td>NEWSLETTER</td><td>LAWS/REGS</td></tr>
<tr><td>♦</td><td>♦</td><td></td><td></td></tr>
<tr><td colspan="2">Includes:
• Disaster Summaries
• Sample Business Contingency Plan
• Earthquake Response Plan
• Tsunami Response Plan
• Business Recovery Manager's Association</td><td colspan="2">• Disaster Recovery Yellow Pages
• Developing a Disaster Recovery Plan
• Geological Hazards
• Weather
• Crisis Communications Strategic Planning
• Virtual Emergency Management Prototype</td></tr>
<tr><td colspan="4"></td></tr>
<tr><td colspan="4">This is a tremendous resource, not just for business planners, but for all planners.</td></tr>
</table>

BUSINESS RECOVERY

Franchise Emergency Action Team (FEAT)			
A consortium of Fortune 500 franchise corporations			
http://www.entremkt.com/feat/			
GRAPHICS	LINKS	NEWSLETTER	LAWS/REGS
	◆		

Includes:
- Feat Flash (updates)
- How to Participate
- Contacting FEAT
- FEAT Facts
- FEAT Guest Book

An unusual resource concept that public sector managers should know about.

U.S. Chamber of Commerce			
U.S. Chamber of Commerce			
http://www.uschamber.org/			
GRAPHICS	LINKS	NEWSLETTER	LAWS/REGS
	◆		◆

Includes:
- Publications
- News and Media Releases
- Issues Information
- What's New
- Programs and Training Services
- Small Business Institute
- Small Business Resources

An important site for emergency managers to find out the needs of business, especially small business, when it comes to planning, response, and recovery.

BUSINESS RECOVERY

Survive!			
Survive!, the business continuity group			
http://www.survive.com			
GRAPHICS	LINKS	NEWSLETTER	LAWS/REGS
	◆		

Includes:
- National Groups and Contacts
- Membership Application
- Key Events
- Professional Development Courses
- Special Interest Groups
- About the Business Continuity Institute
- Key Links

A central location for resources for business disaster recovery and business continuity planning

Business Recovery Manager's Association (BRMA)			
Business Recovery Manager's Association			
http://www.corp.hp.com/publish/brma/			
GRAPHICS	LINKS	NEWSLETTER	LAWS/REGS
	◆		

Includes:
- Meeting Schedules
- Products and Services
- Related Links
- What is Business Recovery Planning
- The Recovery Planning Professional

(BRMA) is a professional organization devoted to the advancement of the theory and practice of business recovery planning, disaster recovery planning and emergency management. Has an exciting mentor program concept.

BUSINESS RECOVERY

Basic Business Recovery Plan			
Massachusetts Institute of Technology			
http://web.mit.edu/security/www/pubplan.htm			
GRAPHICS	LINKS	NEWSLETTER	LAWS/REGS
Includes: A basic text document of a sample disaster recovery plan.			

Disaster Recovery Plan Outline			
University of Toronto			
http://www.utoronto.ca/security/drp.htm#DRP			
GRAPHICS	LINKS	NEWSLETTER	LAWS/REGS
Includes: A basic text document of a sample disaster recovery plan.			

Phoenix Business Disaster Recovery Systems			
Binomial (Vendor)			
http://www.binomial.com/			
GRAPHICS	LINKS	NEWSLETTER	LAWS/REGS
	◆	◆	

Includes:
- Products
- Dealers
- Newsletters
- Screen Shows
- Events/Seminars
- Links

Even though this is a vendor site, you'd better have this one on your page and go to it often. Their free newsletter is very impressive and has the latest hot items.

BUSINESS RECOVERY

Disaster Recovery Information Exchange (DRIE)			
Disaster Recovery Information Exchange			
http://www.drie.org			
GRAPHICS	LINKS	NEWSLETTER	LAWS/REGS
◆	◆		

Includes:	
• Conferences	• Mailing Lists
• Disasters	• Links
	• News

The Disaster Recovery Information Exchange (DRIE) is a non-profit organization dedicated to the promotion of Business Resumption Planning, Computer Recovery, and Crisis Management for business.Great for all around planning of any kind.

CLIMATE

National Climate Data Center			
Dept. of Commerce, NOAA, and National Environmental Satellite, Data, and Information Service (NESDIS)			
http://www.ncdc.noaa.gov			
GRAPHICS	LINKS	NEWSLETTER	LAWS/REGS
◆	◆		

Includes:	
• Search Engine for Climate Information	• Inter-active Visualization of Climate Data
• Products, Publications and Services	• Climate Research Programs
• Data Access	• World Data on Meteorology
• Hot Data Updates	

National Climate Data Center provides information from around the world. Lots of information, photos, articles, links, etc. For drought, flood, and climate changes.

CLIMATE

Global Hydrology and Climate Center			
NASA, University of Alabama, and Universities Space Research Association			
http://wwwghcc.msfc.nasa.gov/			
GRAPHICS	LINKS	NEWSLETTER	LAWS/REGS
	♦		

Includes:
- What's New
- Regional Workshops
- Employment/Research Opportunities
- Seminars
- Chapters

The primary focus of the research center is to understand the Earth's global water cycle, the distribution and variability of atmospheric water, and the impact of human activity as it relates to global and regional climate.

U.S. EPA Global Warming Home Page			
U.S. Environmental Protection Agency			
http://www.epa.gov/globalwarming/home.htm			
GRAPHICS	LINKS	NEWSLETTER	LAWS/REGS
	♦		

Includes:
- Science and Impacts of Global Warming
- Policies and Programs
- Information Sources/Other Links
- Quick Facts
- Latest Developments

For the emergency manager who is looking at long-term planning concerns, especially near coastal areas or areas prone to severe drought.

CLIMATE

Global Hydrology and Climate Center (GHCC) Home Page			
NASA Marshall Space Flight Center			
http://wwwghcc.msfc.nasa.gov/			
GRAPHICS	LINKS	NEWSLETTER	LAWS/REGS
◆	◆		

Includes:
- Who We Are
- What's New
- Calendar of Events
- Visitor Information
- Links to Other Related Sites

The site focuses on the impacts of technology on the environment and has a strong public-private partnership focus.

National Environmental Satellite, Data, and Information Service (NESDIS) Home Page			
National Oceanographic and Atmospheric Administration (NOAA)			
http://ns.noaa.gov/NESDIS/NESDIS_Home.html			
GRAPHICS	LINKS	NEWSLETTER	LAWS/REGS
◆	◆		

Includes:
- Environmental Information Services
- National Oceanographic Data Center
- National Geophysical Data Center
- News
- Links to Other Related Sites

This service can tie emergency managers to the key sites for large-scale climate and satellite study operations.

COMMUNICATIONS

Information on the Convention on the Provision of Telecommunication Resources for Disaster Mitigation and Relief Operations			
Professor Fred Cate: University of Indiana			
http://www.law.indiana.edu/law/disaster/			
GRAPHICS	LINKS	NEWSLETTER	LAWS/REGS
Includes: • Links to Related Sites		• Disaster Communications Documents	
Basic document on telecommunications in disaster.			

The North American Center For Emergency Communications (NACEC) Home Page			
The North American Center For Emergency Communications			
http://www.nacec.org/			
GRAPHICS	LINKS	NEWSLETTER	LAWS/REGS
◆	◆		
Includes: • Disaster Victim Support • Military Family Support		• Specific Event Updates	
Serving Disaster Relief Operations & Military Families. Every emergency planner should know about the services offered by this site, especially when there is a war situation requiring contact with loved ones. They also provide critical communications support for non-profit organizations in disaster.			

COMMUNICATIONS

Coast Guard Navigation Information Center			
Navigation Center (NAVCEN), Coast Guard's Coordination of Radionavigation Management			
http://www.navcen.uscg.mil			
GRAPHICS	LINKS	NEWSLETTER	LAWS/REGS
◆	◆		

Includes:
- Radionavigation Policy Notes
- NAVCEN's Brochure
- GPS
- Boating Safety
- Local Notice to Mariners
- DGPS
- LORAN
- OMEGA
- Chart Ordering Locations
- Marine Communications
- Links to Other Sites

Great place to visit to pick up navigation information and training. Also, lots of information on oil spill protocols, and exercises. Great links and photos.

Navy Marine Corps MARS Telecommunications System National Home Page			
Military Affiliate Radio System			
http://www.maf.mobile.al.us/~navymars/index.html			
GRAPHICS	LINKS	NEWSLETTER	LAWS/REGS
	◆		

Includes:
- What is MARS
- American Radio Relay League(ARRL)
- List of Ships Active in the MARS
- Other WWW MARS Links
- Search Engines

MARS offers a free message system to send MARSGRAMS to and from personnel aboard ships accepting MARSGRAMS, and to a relative or friend in any military service. This is a two-way service for personnel and families back home.

COMPUTER RECOVERY

Disaster Prevention & Recovery Alliance Home Page			
Disaster Prevention & Recovery Alliance			
http://www.dpra.net			
GRAPHICS	LINKS	NEWSLETTER	LAWS/REGS
	♦	♦	

Includes:
- Mission/Objectives
- Benefits and Membership
- Special Events
- News and Notes
- Sponsors

A leading resource, advocate and supporter for emergency management professionals engaged in data protection, remote backup services, and disaster prevention, planning and recovery.

European Contact List for Computer Emergency Response Teams (CERTs)			
DFN-CERT			
http://www.cert.dfn.de/eng/csir/europe/certs.html			
GRAPHICS	LINKS	NEWSLETTER	LAWS/REGS
	♦		

Includes:
- Meetings
- Lists by Country
- Team Member Names

Lists international organizations who respond to attacks on or major losses to computer systems.

COMPUTER RECOVERY

The Computer Emergency Response Team Coordination Center (CERTS)			
Software Engineering Institute of Carnegie Mellon University			
http://www.cert.org/			
GRAPHICS	LINKS	NEWSLETTER	LAWS/REGS

Includes:
- Tutorial
- CERT Advisories
- Archives and Research Information
- Frequently Asked Questions
- Job Postings
- Contact Information

CERTS grew out of work from the Defense Advance Research Projects Agency (DARPA).

EARTHQUAKE

Earthquake Engineering Research Institute (EERI)			
Earthquake Engineering Research Institute			
http://www.eeri.org/			
GRAPHICS	LINKS	NEWSLETTER	LAWS/REGS
◆	◆	◆	◆

Includes:
- About EERI
- News of the Institute
- Online Features
- Audiovisuals
- Timely Information
- Seismic Legislation
- Meeting and Seminars
- Reconnaissance Reports
- Related Links

Perfect for gathering lessons learned from quakes. Not the site for breaking news, but for in-depth follow up. Great briefing docs. Photos. Some links.

EARTHQUAKE

Global Seismology Alert			
British Geological Survey's (BGS) Global Seismology Research Group (GSRG)			
http://www.gsrg.nmh.ac.uk/			
GRAPHICS	LINKS	NEWSLETTER	LAWS/REGS
◆	◆		

Includes:
- Recent Events
- Felt Effects
- Hazards
- Monitoring
- Environment
- European (interests)
- EAP
- Historical Data
- Archives
- Contacts
- About GSRG

Global Earthquake Response Center			
GERC, earthquake.com, earthquake.net, EarthquakeNet, QuakeCam and The Epicenter of the Internet			
http://www.earthquake.com			
GRAPHICS	LINKS	NEWSLETTER	LAWS/REGS
◆	◆	◆	

Includes:
- Online Catalog
- News Stories About Quakes
- Earthquake Links
- Earthquake Forums
- Earthquake Information Search Engine
- Links to News Sites

A very nicely designed site for quality searches for earthquake information and updates.

EARTHQUAKE

National Center for Earthquake Engineering Research (NCEER) University of Buffalo			
http://nceer.eng.buffalo.edu			
GRAPHICS	LINKS	NEWSLETTER	LAWS/REGS
◆	◆		

Includes:
- About NCEER
- Information Assistance
- What's News
- Links to Related Sites
- Publications
- Databases and Software
- Data Resources

Great site. Well designed. Great information. One of best sites. Good photos.

Seismic Assessments for the State of California and other earthquake data			
California Department of Conservation Division of Mines and Geology and U.S. Geological Survey			
http://www.consrv.ca.gov/dmg			
GRAPHICS	LINKS	NEWSLETTER	LAWS/REGS
◆	◆	◆	◆

Includes:
- What's New (usually incredible)
- Mineral Resources Development
- Environmental Review Program
- CDMG Bulletin Board Link
- Links to Other Sites
- Geological Hazards Assessment
- Strong Motion Instrumentation
- Geological Information and Support
- Online Publications

Great site for geological information, especially for earthquake information. Incredible access to maps and publications. Incredible links. A great site.

EARTHQUAKE

Southern California Earthquake Center (SCEC)			
National Science Foundation and the United States Geological Survey			
http://www.usc.edu/dept/earth/quake			
GRAPHICS	LINKS	NEWSLETTER	LAWS/REGS

Includes: • About SCEC • Core Institutions	• SCEC Products • Outreach Programs

This site is still developing. Should be a great site in the future. The Southern California Earthquake Center (SCEC) coordinates research on Los Angeles region earthquake hazards and focuses on applying earth sciences to earthquake hazard reduction. Not much for emergency management yet, but there will be in the future.

Geological Hazards			
US Geological Survey			
http://gldage.cr.usgs.gov			
GRAPHICS	LINKS	NEWSLETTER	LAWS/REGS
◆	◆		

Includes: • Earthquakes • Landslides • Recent Publications • Hazard Images	• Geomagnetism • Other Links • Northridge Earthquake '94 • Bulletin Board • Geological Information (Maps)

This site is a tremendous resource for geological subjects.

EARTHQUAKE

Western States Seismic Policy Council (WSSPC) Home Page				
Western States Seismic Policy Council (WSSPC)				
http://vishnu.glg.nau.edu/wsspc.html				
GRAPHICS	LINKS	NEWSLETTER	LAWS/REGS
◆	◆		

Includes:

- What's New
- Calendar
- Tsunami
- About WSSPC/Membership
- Publications

- Earthquake Links
- Publications
- Earthquake Images/WSSPC Images
- Earthquake Resources
- Search Engine
- Policy Center

Very interesting site. Easy to use. Fascinating list of memberships so you know WHO to contact. Great links. Great Northridge earthquake information.

Association of Bay Area Governments (ABAG) Earthquake and Housing Information				
Association of Bay Area Governments				
http://www.abag.ca.gov/bayarea/eqmaps/eqhouse.html				
GRAPHICS	LINKS	NEWSLETTER	LAWS/REGS
◆	◆		

Includes:

- Excerpts of Documents of Interest
- Viewing Building Impacts

- Mitigation of Housing Problems
- Contractors Guides

Great site. Easy to use. Tons of useful information. Great jump site to other links. Incredible GIS Scenario for EQ damage based on various faults moving.

EARTHQUAKE

GIS in Earthquake Hazard Mapping			
Ian R. Brown, Associates			
http://www.irba.co.nz/pubs/report2.html			
GRAPHICS	LINKS	NEWSLETTER	LAWS/REGS
◆			
Explains one New Zealand approach to using GIS in earthquake hazard mapping. Basically a single article on one use of GIS, with a source for buying the entire report. Useful as one approach to GIS use.			

Museum of City of San Francisco: Earthquake Materials			
Museum of City of San Francisco			
http://www.sfmuseum.org			
GRAPHICS	LINKS	NEWSLETTER	LAWS/REGS
◆	◆		
Includes: • Great Earthquake and Fire of 1906 • 1906 Earthquake Photographs	• 1989 San Francisco Earthquake • San Francisco's Response to the Oakland Firestorm		
Huge source of data and photos on 1906 quake, Loma Prieta, and Oakland Hills Fire. Really worth keeping for resources and talks.			

EARTHQUAKE

San Francisco Fire Department Home Page			
San Francisco Fire Department			
http://www.slip.net/~nertsffd/			
GRAPHICS	LINKS	NEWSLETTER	LAWS/REGS
♦	♦	♦	

Includes:
- NERT Program
- Schedule of NERT Classes
- NERT Student Manual

- NERT Newsletter
- San Francisco Maps
- Historical Data
- Links to Other Sites

Not just fire and earthquake information. Lots of links to related sites. Guide to how the Bay Area Neighborhood Emergency Response Teams (NERTs) are formed and operated.

National Information Service for Earthquake Engineering (NISEE) at the Earthquake Engineering Research Center (EERC)			
University of Berkeley, College of Engineering			
http://www.eerc.berkeley.edu			
GRAPHICS	LINKS	NEWSLETTER	LAWS/REGS
♦	♦		

Includes:
- EQIIS Image Database
- Earthquake Engineering Abstracts
- Computer Applications
- Engineering Reports

- Library
- Seismic Hazard Maps
- Loma Prieta Earthquake
- Kobe Earthquake
- About EERC

For the serious quake researcher. A much improved site with tons of quake data.

EARTHQUAKE

Applied Technology Council (ATC) Home Page			
Applied Technology Council			
http://www.atcouncil.org			
GRAPHICS	LINKS	NEWSLETTER	LAWS/REGS
		◆	

Includes:	
• What's New	• Newsletter
• News Releases	• Technical Briefings
• Building Safety	• Training Manuals
• Building Safety Evaluation Forms	• Databases
	• Seminars and Workshops

A much improved site. An essential research forum for anyone dealing with building issues and earthquake protection and inspection.

The Geophysics Program			
University of Washington			
http://www.geophys.washington.edu			
GRAPHICS	LINKS	NEWSLETTER	LAWS/REGS
◆	◆	◆	

Includes:	
• Pacific Northwest Earthquake Information	• Tsunami Information
• Recent Earthquake List	• The Weekly Planet newsletter
• Cascadia Regional Earthquake Working Group (CREW)	• Seismology and Earthquakes
	• Glaciology
	• Atmospheric and Cloud Geophysics

Seismic surfing gateway to all seismic data and research on the Internet. The premier location for seismology links. A solid research resource on quake activity.

EARTHQUAKE

National Science and Technology Council (NSTC) Home Page			
White House National Science and Technology Council			
http://www.whitehouse.gov/WH/EOP/OSTP/NSTC/html/NSTC_Home.html			
GRAPHICS	LINKS	NEWSLETTER	LAWS/REGS
			♦

Includes:
- Natural Disaster Reduction Plan
- Our Changing Planet (Global Change Research Program)

Site for Strategy for National Earthquake Loss Reduction. Provides a complete copy of the National Earthquake Policy Document. Should be read by all policy makers dealing with earthquake. Very complete.

Induced Earthquake Bibliography			
Darlene A. Cypser, Attorney at Law			
http://www.nyx.net/~dcypser/induceq/induceq.bib.html			
GRAPHICS	LINKS	NEWSLETTER	LAWS/REGS
	♦		

Includes:
- Induced Earthquakes in General
- Injection Induced Earthquakes
- Reservoir Induced Earthquakes
- Oil and Gas Production Induced Quakes
- Mining and Quarrying Induced Quakes
- Nuclear Test Induced Earthquakes
- Seismicity and Underground Gas Storage
- Legal Implications of Induced Quakes
- Links to Related Sites

Very valuable for emergency planners who must deal with people building dams and dumping wastes underground. This bibliography is the largest collection of references on induced seismicity and induced earthquakes.

EMERGENCY ALERT SYSTEM

EAS-Internet			
EAS-net, Dave Biondi			
http://www.eas.net/index.html			
GRAPHICS	LINKS	NEWSLETTER	LAWS/REGS
◆	◆		

Includes:
- Alerts
- Government Agencies
- Private Agencies
- About EAS
- Vendors
- Weather
- Preparation
- System Info and List Servers
- Transition
- E-Chat, E-Store, E-Links
- Media

The only official site for all things associated with the Emergency Alert System which has replaced the Emergency Broadcast System as of January 1, 1996.

EMERGENCY MANAGEMENT

State and Local Emergency Management Data Users Group			
Federal Emergency Management Agency (FEMA)			
http://www.salemdug.dis.anl.gov			
GRAPHICS	LINKS	NEWSLETTER	LAWS/REGS
	◆	◆	

Includes:
- News and Information
- EIIP and FEMA Overview
- Bulletin Board Access
- Internet Links
- PT&E Newsletter Archives (FEMA)
- File Download Area

Home of a wonderful newsletter and a source for emergency management info.

EMERGENCY MANAGEMENT

The EIIP Virtual Forum			
The Emergency Information Infrastructure Partnership			
http://www.emforum.org			
GRAPHICS	LINKS	NEWSLETTER	LAWS/REGS
	◆		◆

Includes:
- Welcome and Site Overview
- Participating Partners
- The Technology Arena
- EIIP Activities
- The Virtual Forum
- The Virtual Library
- The Virtual Classroom
- What's New

This is the beginning of the 21st Century for the emergency management community. This will be the place for emergency managers around the world to meet and share ideas.

Federal Emergency Management Agency (FEMA) Home Page			
FEMA			
http://www.fema.gov			
GRAPHICS	LINKS	NEWSLETTER	LAWS/REGS
◆	◆		◆

Includes:
- What's New
- FEMA News Releases
- Build Safe: Mitigation
- Emergency Preparedness and Training
- Tropical Storm Watch
- Reference Library
- FEMA Top Five Web Sites
- Fire Safety
- Help After Disaster

Great search engines for the site information. Key resource to jump to other sites on the net. This is a key location for all searches.

EMERGENCY MANAGEMENT

Global Emergency Management Service (GEMS) hypertext connection				
Federal Emergency Mangement Agency (FEMA)				
http://femaweb1.fema.gov/cgi-shl/dbml.exe?action=query&template=/gems/g_index.dbm				
GRAPHICS	LINKS	NEWSLETTER	LAWS/REGS	
	◆			
This is an online, searchable database using over 50 categories of Web Sites involved with emergency management. This is a crucial first step for finding emergency management data on the Internet.				

Goddard Space Flight Center List of Best Emergency Management Sites on the Web			
NASA			
http://ltpwww.gsfc.nasa.gov/ndrd/disaster/			
GRAPHICS	LINKS	NEWSLETTER	LAWS/REGS
	◆		
Includes: • Disaster Management • Disciplines	• General • Organizations • Systems •		
Strictly a search engine for emergency management Web Sites. Choices can be by category or by alphabetical search.			

EMERGENCY MANAGEMENT

Emergency Services Database			
District of North Vancouver Fire Services			
http://www.district.north-van.bc.ca/admin/depart/fire/ffsearch/mainmenu.cfm			
GRAPHICS	LINKS	NEWSLETTER	LAWS/REGS
	◆		

Includes:
- Registry
- Data Updates
- Search Engine
- FAQs

- Links to Forums
- Links to E-mail Lists
- Links to Newsgroups
- Links to Air Medical, EMS, Fire, and Search & Rescue

A registry/search site to help people find other emergency management personnel or topics about emergency management. Great site. Something on all topics.

Emergency Management Australia			
Emergency Management, Department of Defense, Australia			
http://www.ema.gov.au/			
GRAPHICS	LINKS	NEWSLETTER	LAWS/REGS
◆	◆		

Includes:
- News and Media
- Australian Emergency Management Institute
- Preparing for Disaster
- Post Disaster

- Education and Training
- Seminars and Conferences
- IDNDR
- Information Services
- EMA Publications and Reports
- National Competency Standards

Very easy to use. Lots of links. A good example of how a government site might be constructed. Clear vision and mission statements up front.

EMERGENCY MANAGEMENT

Emergency Management Gold			
David Crews, Certified Emergency Manager			
http://www.disasters.org/emgold			
GRAPHICS	LINKS	NEWSLETTER	LAWS/REGS
◆	◆		

Includes:	• Resources
• Virtual Library	• State EMAs
• What's New	• Multi-media
• EM Guide	• URLs
• FAQs	• Message Center
• Risks	

Strategic Plan			
Federal Emergency Management Agency (FEMA)			
http://www.fema.gov/nwz97/spln_1.htm			
GRAPHICS	LINKS	NEWSLETTER	LAWS/REGS
	◆		

Includes:
FEMA Strategic Plan for Fiscal Years 1998-2002

This information is critical for all government and public sector emergency planners in order to understand the direction of national policy in emergency management.

EMERGENCY MANAGEMENT

National Coordinating Council on Emergency Management (NCCEM) Definition and Roles			
National Coordinating Council on Emergency Management (NCCEM)			
http://www.nccem.org/			
GRAPHICS	LINKS	NEWSLETTER	LAWS/REGS

Includes:
- About NCCEM
- Committees
- Awards
- Annual Conference
- Topic of the Month
- What's New
- Partners
- Current Issues
- Links to Related Sites

NCCEM is a national organization dedicated to supporting the Emergency Management community. This is a key site for U.S. emergency managers.

National Emergency Management Association (NEMA) Home Page			
National Emergency Management Association (NEMA)			
http://www.nemaweb.org/			
GRAPHICS	LINKS	NEWSLETTER	LAWS/REGS

Includes:
- Regional Communications
- Publications
- Committees
- Educational Programs in Emergency Management
- NEMA HMGP Database
- Membership
- Legislative and Federal Issue Tracking
- State Contact Information
- Research Information

The fastest site to find out which state leaders are tackling problems in emergency management, and the development of national policy based on state actions.

EMERGENCY MANAGEMENT

Emergency Net			
Emergency Response and Research Institute (ERRI)			
http://www.emergency.com			
GRAPHICS	LINKS	NEWSLETTER	LAWS/REGS
◆	◆		

Includes:	Military Operations Page
• Emergency Services Graphics	• Infectious Disease
• Police Operations	• Counter-Terrorism Operations
• Fire Operations	• Management, Computers, Future
• EMS Operations	• ERRI Assessment/Safety
• Disaster /Rescue Operations	• Book Reviews and Order Forms
• Hazardous Materials Operations	• Emergency News Service

One of the best Web Sites. Packed full of useful information for fire, police and emergency medical services. Well designed and thought out. Great photos and links.

American Public Works Association (APWA) Council On Emergency Management Home Page			
American Public Works Association (APWA)			
http://ltpwww.gsfc.nasa.gov/geowarn/dbtoc/project0011.html			
GRAPHICS	LINKS	NEWSLETTER	LAWS/REGS
	◆		

Includes:	• Membership
• Purpose	• Projects
• Mission	• Contacts

Just a brief page defining their operation, but critical for understanding their role.

EMERGENCY MANAGEMENT

Ada City-County Emergency Management Home Page			
Ada City-County Emergency Management			
http://netnow.micron.net/~accem			

GRAPHICS	LINKS	NEWSLETTER	LAWS/REGS
	♦		

Includes:
- 4 Phases of Emergency Plans
- Flash Flood Information
- Ada County Hazards
- Ada County Emergency Plans
- Exercises and Training
- Family Emergency Preparedness
- Emergency Preparedness Pointers

A local emergency management agency in Boise, Idaho. Useful as a link to other local emergency agency home pages. Does exactly what it is supposed to do. Simple layout. Easy to use and understand. Good example of how local government could use the Internet to show how it plans for disaster.

EMERGENCY SUPPLIES

Emergency Products Kits Home Page			
EPK (vendor)			
http://www.epks.com/			

GRAPHICS	LINKS	NEWSLETTER	LAWS/REGS
♦		♦	

Includes:
- Products
- Fund Raiser Programs
- Preparedness Information Center
- EPK Newsletter

Good site for anyone interested in purchasing survival kits for set periods, and different needs. Also features emergency news.

EMERGENCY SUPPLIES

Handi-Links To Emergency Supplies Home Page			
Handilinks			
http://www.ahandyguide.com/cat1/e/e212.htm			
GRAPHICS	LINKS	NEWSLETTER	LAWS/REGS
	◆		

Includes:	• Food Systems
• Medical Supplies	• Communications Equipment
• Earthquake Supplies	• Home and Office Kits

The page for finding vendors of disaster equipment. Limited but valuable.

ENVIRONMENT

U.S. Fish and Wildlife Service Home Page			
U.S. Fish and Game			
http://www.fws.gov			
GRAPHICS	LINKS	NEWSLETTER	LAWS/REGS
◆	◆		

Includes:	• Help
• Who We Are	• Search Engine
• What We Do	• News (also provides information
• Where We Are	in Spanish)

Definitely worth a look when federal wildlands are impacted in disaster. One of best organized lists of links. Very nice site. Has a great search engine. Lots of risk assessment documentation.

ENVIRONMENT

Information for a Changing World			
Consortium for International Earth Science Information Network			
http://hdpdis.info@hdp.org/			
GRAPHICS	LINKS	NEWSLETTER	LAWS/REGS
◆	◆		

Includes:
- Interactive Applications
- Metadata Resources
- Data Resources
- Information Systems and Resources
- Information Cooperative
- Education and Training
- Services
- Programs
- Job Opportunities

Excellent jumping off point to a myriad of emergency sites related to earth global and environmental issues, including those that impact large-scale emergency management concerns.

United Nations Environmental Programs Home Page			
United Nations			
http://www.unep.or.jp/ietc/index.html#Guide			
GRAPHICS	LINKS	NEWSLETTER	LAWS/REGS
◆	◆	◆	

Includes:
- Search Engine by Key Word
- What's New
- News and Events
- Projects
- Newsletter and Publications
- Comments and Suggestions

This is a great place for hazmat planners, or general planners concerned about environmental issues, to find data to back their decision making.

ENVIRONMENT

U.S. Environmental Protection Agency (EPA) Home Page			
U.S. Environmental Protection Agency			
http://www.epa.gov/			
GRAPHICS	LINKS	NEWSLETTER	LAWS/REGS
◆	◆		◆

Includes:
- EPA Strategic Plan
- Business and Industry Section
- Government Section
- Programs and Initiatives
- Contracts, Grants and Financing
- EPA News
- Regulations
- Publications
- Data Systems and Software

Incredible source of information. First place to stop for environmental research.

FIRE

National Fire Protection Academy (NFPA) Home Page			
National Fire Protection Academy			
http://www.nfpa.org			
GRAPHICS	LINKS	NEWSLETTER	LAWS/REGS
◆	◆		◆

Includes:
- NFPA Codes and Standards
- Proposals (comments and queries)
- Calendars and Meetings
- Fire Safety Information
- Search Engine
- What's New
- New Releases
- Periodicals
- Links to Other Sites

Great site for basic fire information and standards. Everyone in fire service or dealing with fire planning should use this. Great reports, resources, and contacts.

FIRE

Wildfire Magazine Home Page			
International Association of Wildland Fire (IAWF) monthly bulletin			
http://www.neotecinc.com/wildfire			
GRAPHICS	LINKS	NEWSLETTER	LAWS/REGS
	◆	◆	

Includes:
- What's New
- News Alerts
- Database Search

- Wildfire Safety Articles
- Incident Reporting
- Fire Accident Investigations
- Links to Other Sites

A constantly improving site with information critical to the emergency planner with serious wildland-urban interface concerns.

Firewise Home Page			
National Firewise Landscaping Task Force			
http://www.firewise.org/			
GRAPHICS	LINKS	NEWSLETTER	LAWS/REGS
	◆		

Includes:
- Firewise Features
- Fire Fuelish Features
- Calendar of Events
- Event Registration

- Slope in Terrain
- Fuel
- Roof
- Defensible Space
- Links

Great site for basic information for people at risk for fire throughout North America. Lots of good links.

FIRE

Wildfire Hazard Information and Mitigation System (WHIMS)			
Boulder County, Colorado			
http://www.boco.co.gov/gislu/whims.html			
GRAPHICS	LINKS	NEWSLETTER	LAWS/REGS
◆	◆		

Includes:
- Basic Information
- Project Summary
- Defensible Space
- Sample Maps
- Posters
- Wildfire Photos
- Links to City/County Government

Very focused on local Colorado fire issues, but this site has great links to other sites, and an impressive use of GIS for a specific application.

FLOOD

Automated Local Evaluation in Real Time (ALERT) Flood Warning System			
Automated Local Evaluation in Real Time			
http://www.io.com/~rooke/alert			
GRAPHICS	LINKS	NEWSLETTER	LAWS/REGS
◆	◆		

Includes:
- Benefits
- ALERT History
- User's Group
- News of Interest
- ALERT Vendors
- Want Ads
- Feedback

Basically a vendor site for gathering field data from remote sensors.

FLOOD

The NOAA NESDIS ORA Flash Flood Home Page			
National Oceanic and Atmospheric Administration (NOAA)			
http://orbit-net.nesdis.noaa.gov/ora/ht/ff			
GRAPHICS	LINKS	NEWSLETTER	LAWS/REGS
	◆		

Includes:
- Automated Precipitation Products
- Blended Precipitation Water and Forecast Products
- Soil Wetness Index Products
- Links to Related Sites

Superb site for finding some of the latest information on monitoring conditions for flash flooding. This site focuses on products for flash flood forecasting.

California Department of Water Resources Home Page			
California Department of Water Resources			
http://www.dwr.water.ca.gov/			
GRAPHICS	LINKS	NEWSLETTER	LAWS/REGS

Includes:
- About DWR
- What's New
- California Water Map
- Water Conditions
- California Water Information
- State Water Project
- Search Engine and Index

This site is invaluable for anyone dealing with emergency planning for water issues in California, including states adjoining California that are impacted by shared watersheds.

FLOOD

Flood Hazard Research Center			
Middlesex University, Great Britain, School of Geography and Environmental Management			
http://www.mdx.ac.uk/www/gem/fhrc.htm			
GRAPHICS	LINKS	NEWSLETTER	LAWS/REGS

Includes:
- Undergraduate Courses
- Post Graduate Courses
- Research
- Seminars and Conferences
- Publications
- Alumni
- Services

Another site offering a degree in emergency management. The center studies the interaction between people and the environment, analyzes environmental policy, and provides teaching and training. Most information is focused on flood activities. There are basic texts with contacts to key investigators.

Global Flood Monitoring and Analysis Project			
Dartmouth College			
http://www.dartmouth.edu/artsci/geog/floods/Index.html			
GRAPHICS	LINKS	NEWSLETTER	LAWS/REGS
♦	♦		

Includes:
- Annual Flood Information and Anomalies
- Running Tallies of Flood Damage
- Enhanced Flood Images
- Image Files for 1995 California Flooding
- Current Flooding Information
- Weekly Flood Maps and Data
- Flood Remote Sensing Reference

This site is a heavy user of satellite imagery. It's one of the first places to get flood data/history. Great maps and graphics! Very easy to use.

FLOOD

U.S. Bureau of Reclamation Home Page			
U.S. Bureau of Reclamation: Department of the Interior			
http://www.usbr.gov/			
GRAPHICS	LINKS	NEWSLETTER	LAWS/REGS
	◆		

Includes:
- Mission and Vision Statement
- Commissioner
- GPRA plan
- Phone numbers
- The Book *Introduction to Reclamation*
- Search Engine

Focuses on water conservation, treatment, quality, supply and uses, and managing water-related resources west of the Mississippi River.

U.S. Corps of Engineers Home Page			
U.S. Corps of Engineers			
http://www.usace.army.mil/			
GRAPHICS	LINKS	NEWSLETTER	LAWS/REGS

Includes:
- What We Do
- Information
- News
- Organization
- Search Engine
- Help Tools
- Strategic Plan

Valuable site for emergencies surrounding federal reservoirs and dams.

FLOOD

Real-Time Water Data			
U.S. Geological Survey (USGS)			
http://h2o.usgs.gov/public/realtime.html			
GRAPHICS	LINKS	NEWSLETTER	LAWS/REGS
◆	◆		

Includes:
- Status Notes
- Weather
- Water
- Data
- Key Links to Other Sites
- NWIS
- Quality
- Use
- Acid Rain

Site for reports on current streamflow conditions, and in many states, hydrographs of streamflows. A key allows you to choose by state, and takes you right to the stream flow indicators. Very useful before and during floods.

Trinity River Information Network			
North Central Texas Council of Governments (NCTCOG)			
http://www.nctcog.dst.tx.us:80/envir/trin/trinity.html			
GRAPHICS	LINKS	NEWSLETTER	LAWS/REGS
◆	◆		

Includes:
- Special News and Additions
- Trinity River Basin Basic Information
- Search Engine
- Trinity River Common Vision Program
- Trinity River Related Information
- Examples Across the Nation and World

A way for central Texas communities and government to work on flood plain issues in the open forum of the Internet. A boiler plate for public/government partnership.

FLOOD

Flood Control District of Maricopa County, Arizona				
Flood Control District of Maricopa County, Arizona				
http://www.maricopa.gov/flood/fcd.html				
GRAPHICS	LINKS	NEWSLETTER	LAWS/REGS	
◆	◆			

Includes:
- About the District and Flood Control Board
- Completed Projects
- Flood Alert Page

- Flood Readiness
- Public Meeting Schedules
- Annual Report
- District Software
- Links to Other Sites

This site is maintained by a water district providing services to the community, including warnings for flooding. A good site for seeing how government can reach out and touch the public it serves and provide valuable add-on services like warnings for disaster.

Federal Energy Regulatory Commission (FERC) Home Page				
Federal Energy Regulatory Commission				
http://www.ferc.fed.us/				
GRAPHICS	LINKS	NEWSLETTER	LAWS/REGS	
◆	◆		◆	

Includes:
- Public Reference Room
- Natural Gas
- Oil

- Electricity
- Hydroelectricity
- Office of External Affairs
- Bulletin Board System

Useful site when planning for utility operations, especially federal dams.

GENERAL TOPICS

Emergency Net News Service			
Emergency Response & Research Institute			
http://www.emergency.com/			
GRAPHICS	LINKS	NEWSLETTER	LAWS/REGS
◆	◆	◆	

Includes:
- Graphics
- Police Operations
- Fire Operations
- EMS Operations
- Disaster/Rescue Operations
- Hazardous Materials Operations
- Military Operations
- Infectious Diseases
- Counter-Terrorism Operations
- Management, Computers, Future
- Safety

NASA Ames Research Emergency Communications Center (*StoneFly*)			
National Aeronautics and Space Administration (NASA)			
http://stonefly.arc.nasa.gov/			
GRAPHICS	LINKS	NEWSLETTER	LAWS/REGS
	◆	◆	

Includes:
- Emergency Organizations
- FEMA Bulletins
- Weather Updates
- Earthquake Reports
- Membership Database Search
- Emergency Video-Conferencing
- E-mail Project Manager

A developing site with fantastic future capabilities and resources for the emergency management community. It offers a newletter as part of the StoneFly Project.

GENERAL TOPICS

CNN Crisis Center			
CNN Television			
http://www.cnn.com/CRISIS/index.html			
GRAPHICS	LINKS	NEWSLETTER	LAWS/REGS
◆	◆		

Includes:
- Breaking News
- Headlines
- Summaries

CNN has used this site as an open update location for breaking events.

Eye on the World: Our Violent Planet			
Ken Roe			
http://www.iwaynet.net/~kwroejr/violent.html			
GRAPHICS	LINKS	NEWSLETTER	LAWS/REGS
	◆		

Includes:
- General
- Earthquakes
- Fire
- Volcanoes
- Weather-Related

A take-off point for all kinds of other emergency sites, based on topics listed above, in subgroups.

GENERAL TOPICS

Center of Excellence in Disaster Management and Humanitarian Assistance (COE)			
Tripler Army Medical Center			
http://coe.tamc.amedd.army.mil/			
GRAPHICS	LINKS	NEWSLETTER	LAWS/REGS
♦	♦		

Includes:	• Virtual Library
• What's New	• Education Training
• Current Disasters	• Asia-Pacific

Focus is the Asia-Pacific Region, but this site has a little of everything for the emergency manager. Critical for finding ways to develop civilian-military coordination for disaster response/recovery. This site has a huge Web Site link database.

Caribbean Disaster Emergency Response Agency (CDERA) part of Caribbean Community (CARICOM)			
Pan Caribbean Disaster Preparedness and Prevention Project (PCDPPP)			
http://www.cdera.org/members.htm			
GRAPHICS	LINKS	NEWSLETTER	LAWS/REGS
♦	♦		

Includes:	• About CDERA
• Eligibility	• Calendar of Events
• National Disaster Coordinators List	• Links

A critical site for planning in the Caribbean; for agencies coordinating emergency response with that region.

GENERAL TOPICS

Hazard Net : International Decade for Natural Disaster Reduction (IDNDR) Demonstration Project			
Simon Fraser University			
http://hoshi.cic.sfu.ca/hazard			

GRAPHICS	LINKS	NEWSLETTER	LAWS/REGS
◆	◆		

Includes:

- Hazard Warnings, Alerts, Advisories
- Recent Hazard Impacts
- Operations Background
- Emergency Organizations

- Monitoring Programs
- Early Warning Systems
- Internet Search Engine
- Hazard Information Subsystems (covers most emergency management topics)

Great jump site. It mainly leads the reader to other places. Has a useful Internet search engine. Site is divided into operational and informational services.

The Disaster Connection			
Gisli Olafson			
http://www.itn.is/~gro/disaster/			

GRAPHICS	LINKS	NEWSLETTER	LAWS/REGS
◆	◆		

Includes:

- Links

- Updates

Great site for connecting to other places, but this site is not updated very often. Has some other good information and articles, but limited. A great index, included in this document. Under construction—could be the best with some work.

GENERAL TOPICS

Earthweek
Steve Newman
http://www.slip.net/~earthenv/

GRAPHICS	LINKS	NEWSLETTER	LAWS/REGS
◆		◆	

Includes:
- Weekly Updates of Disasters
- Back Issues
- Maps of Worldwide Disasters

Great for information updates from April 1996. Good background for disasters during that period. Uses a unique mapping system to designate where certain disasters have occurred. Well constructed and useful. Graphically stunning.

Growing Smart Home Page
Growing Smart Project
http://www.planning.org/plnginfo/GROWSMAR/outline.html

GRAPHICS	LINKS	NEWSLETTER	LAWS/REGS
	◆		◆

Includes:
- Initiating Planning Statute Reform
- Purposes and Grant of Power
- Definitions
- State Planning
- State Land-Use Control
- Regional Planning
- Tax Equity and Tax Relief

This site is the home of the Legislative Guidebook to help those concerned with planning for land development and regional development. Very helpful for today's emergency manager.

GEOLOGY

National Geophysical Data Center (NGDC)			
Solid Earth Geophysics, Boulder, Colorado			
http://www.ngdc.noaa.gov/seg/hazard/ hazards.html			
GRAPHICS	LINKS	NEWSLETTER	LAWS/REGS
◆			

Includes:
- Natural Hazards Slides
- Earthquake Data and Publications
- Tsunami Data and Publications
- World Stress Data
- Natural Hazards Data Resources

Great pictures, but no links. Had some nice slide sets for sale.

California Resources Agency Environmental Information by Geographic Area			
California Environmental Resources Evaluation System (CERES) Environmental Information by Geographic Region: California			
http://ceres.ca.gov/geo.html			
GRAPHICS	LINKS	NEWSLETTER	LAWS/REGS
◆	◆		

Includes: (county information)
- Economics and Demographics
- Environmental Groups and Projects
- Governmental Institutions
- Land Use Planning
- Recreational Resources
- Water Resources
- Road and Weather Conditions
- Special Status Species
- Vegetation and Habitats
- Maps and Spatial Data
- Photos and Satellite Imagery

A very unusual way to track information for planning purposes in California. The site immediately lets you search graphically by county or by bioregion.

GEOLOGY

U.S. Geological Survey (USGS) Home Page			
U.S. Geological Survey			
http://www.usgs.gov			
GRAPHICS	LINKS	NEWSLETTER	LAWS/REGS
♦	♦		

Includes:
- About USGS
- Contacts
- Publications and Data
- Fact Sheets
- Search Engine
- How to Use the Web Resources
- Sections on Hazards, the Environment, Natural Resources, and Information Management

A wonderful general site to pick up information for many planning purposes. A planner should spend at least an hour exploring what this site offers.

GAIA Alert Home Page			
Millenium Matters			
http://www.m-m.org/jz/gaia.html			
GRAPHICS	LINKS	NEWSLETTER	LAWS/REGS
	♦		

Includes:
- Geology Alert
- Weather Alert
- Environmental Alert
- Oceans Alert
- Celestial Alert
- Preparation Checklist
- How to Help the Earth

An non-professional focus on world-wide disasters. Odd, but disaster summaries are okay.

GOVERNMENT

Fed World Information Network			
U.S. Department of Commerce, National Technical Information Service			
http://www.fedworld.gov			
GRAPHICS	LINKS	NEWSLETTER	LAWS/REGS
	◆		

Includes:
- Search Engines for Federal Web Sites
- General Information Services
- FedWorld-Hosted Web Sites
- Further Information
- Search US Government Information Sources

A must-have site in your bookmarks. A gateway to all federal offices. Great search tools. A first stop to do research and locate items in the U.S. Federal government.

The Federal Web Locator			
Villanova Center for Information Law and Policy			
http://www.law.vill.edu/fed-agency/fedwebloc.html			
GRAPHICS	LINKS	NEWSLETTER	LAWS/REGS
◆	◆		

Includes:
- Search by Agency Name
- Latest Links
- Quick Jumps
- Table of Contents
- Links to Other Search Engines

One of the hottest research starting points on the Web to find anything on the federal side of U.S. government. This should be a bookmark in every emergency manager's computer.

GOVERNMENT

Consumer Information Center (CIC)			
U.S. Consumer Information Service			
http://www.pueblo.gsa.gov			
GRAPHICS	LINKS	NEWSLETTER	LAWS/REGS
◆	◆		

Includes:
- What's New
- Search Engine
- Links to Other Sites
- Consumer News
- Downloadable Catalogs
- Specific topic areas for federal programs, money, small business, health, environment, housing, and miscellaneous topics

Critical for finding the right stuff from the feds in print to be used for educating the public about issues tied to emergency planning, both community and personal.

State of California Governor's Office of Emergency Services			
State of California			
http://www.oes.ca.gov/			
GRAPHICS	LINKS	NEWSLETTER	LAWS/REGS
◆	◆	◆	◆

Includes:
- Flood and Storm Information
- Facts About OES
- Emergency Public Information
- California State Emergency Plan
- OES Departments
- Related Agencies
- Search Engine

A good site for connections for emergency management information, both specific to California and general.

GOVERNMENT

Council of State Governments Home Page			
Council of State Governments			
http://www.csg.org/			
GRAPHICS	LINKS	NEWSLETTER	LAWS/REGS
	◆	◆	◆

Includes:
- Issue Alerts
- What's New
- Upcoming Events
- State Information Packets
- State Information Center
- Publications Catalog
- State Government Officials
- Press Releases
- State Government News
- Health Policy Monitor
- Suggested Legislation

Government emergency planners should visit this site no less than once a month.

National League of Cities Home Page			
National League of Cities (NLC)			
http://www.nlc.org/			
GRAPHICS	LINKS	NEWSLETTER	LAWS/REGS
	◆		

Includes:
- About NLC
- State Leagues
- Local Government
- State Government
- Federal Government
- Public Policy
- General Research
- Search the Web
- Miscellaneous

This is a critical site for anyone planning for emergency management issues that involve cities. It is also a wonderful jump site to other critical links, including *Fountainhead*, which allows you to search County Title Records all over the U.S.

HAZARDOUS MATERIALS

1996 Emergency Response Guidebook (NAERG) (US DOT)for Windows			
Test Depth Software, Idaho			
http://www.testdepth.com/naerg.htm			
GRAPHICS	LINKS	NEWSLETTER	LAWS/REGS

Includes:
- Searchable Chemical Database
- Create Reports
- Print Report Results
- Import Maps
- View and Print NAERG Text

All planners should have this on their desktops if they plan response. Here's how to get a copy of the response plan for windows (a free tour is on the Web Site). This is a vendor site.

EPA's Chemical Emergency Preparedness and Prevention Office (CEPPO)			
United States Environmental Protection Agency			
http://www.epa.gov/swercepp/			
GRAPHICS	LINKS	NEWSLETTER	LAWS/REGS
	◆		◆

Includes:
- What's New
- Upcoming Events
- Publications
- Legislation/Regulations
- Accident Histories
- Electronic Tools
- Outside Resources
- Accident Prevention and Risk
- Right to Know
- Emergency Response
- Chemical Information

All those involved with chemical disaster planning must learn to use this site.

HAZARDOUS MATERIALS

Hazardous Materials Management Magazine Home Page			
Hazardous Materials Management			
http://www.hazmatmag.com/			
GRAPHICS	LINKS	NEWSLETTER	LAWS/REGS
◆	◆		

Includes:
- Environmental Directory and Buyer Guide
- Library/Resources
- What's New
- Links to Key Vendors
- Software/Multimedia Supplement

This Canadian site should be in every hazardous materials planner's bookmark sites. A great place to go. Wonderful links. Great articles.

Lawrence Livermore National Laboratory 's Environmental Compliance Manual. 10.0 Product Storage/Hazardous Materials. Contents. 10.1 Inventory Requirements. 10.1.1, Regulatory Summary. 10.1.2.			
Lawrence Livermore National Laboratory			
http://www.llnl.gov/es_and_h/ecm/chapter_10/chap10.html			
GRAPHICS	LINKS	NEWSLETTER	LAWS/REGS

Includes:
- Inventory Requirements
- Petroleum Underground and Aboveground Storage Tanks
- Hazardous Materials Transportation
- Hazardous Materials Storage

A ready made compliance manual for hazmat planners.

HAZARDOUS MATERIALS

Conservation and Environmental Protection - Internet Links			
University of California, Davis			
http://ice.ucdavis.edu/Cyberspace_Jump_Station/environmental_protection/toxic_and_hazardous_materials.html			
GRAPHICS	LINKS	NEWSLETTER	LAWS/REGS
♦	♦		♦

Includes:	
• Indexes of Bibliographies for Life Science, Environmental Politics, and Life Sciences • News Items	• Current Events and Conferences • Toxic and Hazardous Materials • Pesticide Data Submitters List • Toxic Releases Inventory (TRI) 1993 GIS Maps by State

Gets a hazmat planner to key toxic materials and hazmat sites.

HEALTH/MEDICAL

Pan American Health Organization (PAHO) emergency management for Latin America			
PAHO: Pan American Sanitary Bureau, Regional Office of WHO			
http://www.paho.org			
GRAPHICS	LINKS	NEWSLETTER	LAWS/REGS
♦	♦	♦	

Includes:	
• Quick Reference List—Site Index • Search Engine • Technical Information	• Country Health Profiles • Publications • Library Services • Links to Related Sites

Features the newsletter *Disasters: Preparedness and Mitigation in the Americas.*

HEALTH/MEDICAL

Epidemiological International Bulletins (EPO)			
World Health Organization (WHO)			
http://www.cdc.gov/epo/mmwr/international/world.html			
GRAPHICS	LINKS	NEWSLETTER	LAWS/REGS
	◆		

Includes:
- Search Engine Based on a World Map
- WHO Weekly Epidemiological Record
- Health Bulletins from New Independent States of the Former Soviet Union

Plenty of updated material on latest disease situations and outbreaks.

Medical Encyclopedia Demo			
Mosby Consumer Health			
http://www.ami-med.com/mhc/main.htm			
GRAPHICS	LINKS	NEWSLETTER	LAWS/REGS

Includes:
- Diseases
- Symptoms
- Drugs
- Drug Intervention
- Special Topics
- Nutrition
- Surgeries
- Special Topics
- Common Injuries
- Hot News in Medicine
- Search Engine

Medical demo useful for setting up medical scenarios for exercises and drills.

HEALTH/MEDICAL

MedicCom.Org			
Center for Disaster Education and Research			
http://mediccom.org/public/default.htm			
GRAPHICS	LINKS	NEWSLETTER	LAWS/REGS
	◆		

Includes:	
• Toledo Area Disaster Medical Assistance Team • Center for Disaster Education and Research • Disaster of the Month	• Links to Other Disaster Sites • Mailing Lists • Disaster FTP Site Library • Other Direct Links for Medical Information

This site is critical for medical planning in emergency management. MedicCom BBS is the nation's largest Public Safety and Disaster Management Bulletin Board System. Through this WWW connection to the BBS, you can download files and read public messages.

Morbidity and Mortality Weekly Report			
U.S. Center for Disease Control (CDC)			
http://www.cdc.gov/epo/mmwr/mmwr.html			
GRAPHICS	LINKS	NEWSLETTER	LAWS/REGS
	◆	◆	

Includes:	
• Morbidity and Mortality Report • Bulletins from Around the World • Recommendations and Reports	• Search Engine • Surveillance Summaries • Supplements • Summary of Notifiable Diseases

This is a critical site for data.

HEALTH/MEDICAL

Medicine and Global Survival Magazine Home Page			
Designated Journal of the International Physicians for the Prevention of Nuclear War (IPPNW)			
http://www.healthnet.org/MGS/MGS.html			

GRAPHICS	LINKS	NEWSLETTER	LAWS/REGS
	◆		

Includes:
- Frequently Asked Questions
- Overview
- Mission
- Current Articles
- News Section

- Editorials
- Calendar
- Archives
- The M&GS Annex
- Editorial Board and Author Instructions
- Links to Other Web Sites

This journal prints cutting edge articles on any disease, vector, tool of war or technology, or any other source that may have medical implications to health.

U.S. National Library of Medicine Search Engine			
National Institutes of Health (NIH)			
http://www.nlm.nih.gov/			

GRAPHICS	LINKS	NEWSLETTER	LAWS/REGS
	◆	◆	

Includes:
- Hot Topics
- News
- Databases and Electronic Information

- Other Publications
- Free MEDLINE Access
- Search Engine
- Health Information

This is a critical site for emergency managers to get the latest medical data.

HEALTH/MEDICAL

Global Health Disaster Network Home Page			
Updated by Department of Emergency Medicine, Ehime University School of Medicine, Ehime University, Ehime, Japan			
http://hypnos.m.ehime-u.ac.jp/GHDNet/index.html			
GRAPHICS	LINKS	NEWSLETTER	LAWS/REGS
	♦	♦	
Includes: • Global Health Disaster Network • World Association for Disaster and Emergency Medicine		• Cardiopulmonary Resuscitation • Japanese Association for Acute Medicine • Disaster-Related Information	
This site features the newsletter of World Association of Disaster and Emergency Medicine (WADEM). Has some great "lessons learned" pages, and the WADEM newsletter has lots of good information. Also features a Japanese version.			

HURRICANE

Fact Sheets on Hurricanes			
Federal Emergency Management Agency (FEMA)			
http://www.fema.gov/fema/hurricaf.html			
GRAPHICS	LINKS	NEWSLETTER	LAWS/REGS
	♦		
Includes: • Before and During a Hurricane Watch • During a Hurricane Warning		• After: Inspection and Mitigation • Inspecting Utilities in a Damaged Home	
Good content and valuable for managers who need brief, concise guidelines.			

HURRICANE

Federal Emergency Management Agency (FEMA) Tropical Storm Watch page			
Federal Emergency Management Agency (FEMA)			
http://www.fema.gov/fema/trop.html			
GRAPHICS	LINKS	NEWSLETTER	LAWS/REGS
◆	◆		

Includes:
- Advisories Index
- Reports Index
- Helpful Information Index

A huge base of information on tropical storms that is easy to use. Very focused. Great graphics and links.

National Hurricane Center Tropical Prediction Center			
National Center for Environmental Prediction			
http://www.nhc.noaa.gov			
GRAPHICS	LINKS	NEWSLETTER	LAWS/REGS
◆	◆		

Includes:
- Archives of previous year's hurricanes
- Latest Forecast
- Satellite and Radar Imagery
- Latest Reconnaissance Data
- Information About the Center
- What's New
- Site Maps

Any planner on the U.S. East and Southern Coast, or the Caribbean, should be monitoring this site carefully.

HURRICANE

Ft. Lauderdale's Sun Sentinel Hurricane Home Page
Ft. Lauderdale's Sun Sentinel
http://www.sun-sentinel.com/storm/

GRAPHICS	LINKS	NEWSLETTER	LAWS/REGS
♦	♦		

Includes:
- Preparation
- History
- Tracking Maps
- Quiz
- Latest Updates
- Links to Other Sites
- Local Weather

Newspaper home page for weather in Florida; and also describes how to prepare for and recover from hurricanes.

Coastal Hazards Assessment and Mitigation Project (CHAMP), and Wind Load Facility (X) Home Page
Clemson University, South Carolina
http://champ.eng.clemson.edu/

GRAPHICS	LINKS	NEWSLETTER	LAWS/REGS
♦	♦		

Includes:
- Brief History
- WLTF Projects
- Links to Sponsor Sites
- CHAMP Faculty
- Hazard Mitigation Courses
- Interdisciplinary Thrust Area (ITA)
- Links to Sites for Hurricane, Tropical, and Severe Storms
- Link to National Weather Service

Wonderful hurricane history file data. Lots of photos.

INSURANCE

Winds and Other Perils, State Farm Insurance Home Page			
State Farm Insurance			
http://www.statefarm.com/educate/brochure.htm#wind			
GRAPHICS	LINKS	NEWSLETTER	LAWS/REGS

Includes:	
• Earthquake: Are You Ready	• No Frozen Pipes
• Ice Dams	• Tornado: Plan to Survive
	• You Are at Risk (From Wildfire)

This is the home page for insurance vendor, State Farm, offering useful brochures and information. Useful site for additional materials for training and education.

Insurance Institute for Property Loss Reduction			
Insurance Institute for Property Loss Reduction (IIPLR)			
http://www.bus.orst.edu/FACULTY/NIELSON/AV/iiplr.htm			
GRAPHICS	LINKS	NEWSLETTER	LAWS/REGS
Address for obtaining videotapes on property loss reduction.			

INSURANCE

American Risk and Insurance Association (ARIA) Home Page
American Risk and Insurance Association (ARIA)
http://www.aria.org/

GRAPHICS	LINKS	NEWSLETTER	LAWS/REGS
	◆	◆	

Includes:
- What Is ARIA
- News and Announcements
- RTSWeb—Risk Theory
- ARIA Journals (with links)
- Academic Risk and Insurance Webs
- Other Risk and Insurance Webs
- Search Engine

The purpose of ARIA Web is to provide information concerning the programs and services offered to members and friends of the American Risk and Insurance Association. Good place for the planner to go for information on the private sector insurance industry activities.

The Chubb Corporation: Insurance Library
The Chubb Corporation
http://www.chubb.com/library/

GRAPHICS	LINKS	NEWSLETTER	LAWS/REGS
◆	◆		

Includes:
- Periodicals
- Business
- Home

Very useful site, not just for insurance, but for documents and guidance for business and the general public. Very well constructed, with many links to other useful insurance sites.

LANDSLIDE

U.S. Geological Survey National Landslide Information Center Home Page			
U.S. Geological Survey			
http://gldage.cr.usgs.gov/html_files/nlicsun.html			
GRAPHICS	LINKS	NEWSLETTER	LAWS/REGS
◆			

Includes:
- State Information for Landslides
- Landslide Highlights
- Interesting Landslide Topics
- Announcements, Meetings, Seminars
- Landslide Publications
- Images of Landslides
- Link to Geological Hazard Team

This is the premier site for information on landslides.

LAW ENFORCEMENT

Crime Link Sites			
Yahoo			
http://www.yahoo.com/Society_and_Culture/Crime/			
GRAPHICS	LINKS	NEWSLETTER	LAWS/REGS
	◆		

Includes:
A complete listing of sites dealing with law enforcement issues.

Any incredibly easy way to find out the latest details and numbers on the latest crimes, trends, and areas of interest like asset confiscation, correction and rehabilitation, gangs, death penalty, missing persons, victim's rights, etc.

LAW ENFORCEMENT

The Intelligence Community Home Page			
Headed by CIA, includes Defense Intelligence Agency, National Security Agency, National Reconnaissance Office, The Central Imagery Office, Army- Naval- Marine Corp- Air Force Intelligence Agencies, Department of State, Department of Energy, Treasury, FBI			
http://www.odci.gov/ic			
GRAPHICS	LINKS	NEWSLETTER	LAWS/REGS
	◆		

Includes:	• What's New
• Who We Are	• Links to All Agencies

Gives a basic background, and describes studies to improve the U.S. Intelligence Community. Also links to all of the intelligence agency home pages.

Bureau of Alcohol Tobacco and Firearms Home Page			
Bureau of Alcohol Tobacco and Firearms (BATF)			
http://atf.ustreas.gov/			
GRAPHICS	LINKS	NEWSLETTER	LAWS/REGS
◆	◆	◆	

Includes:	• Firearms
• What's New	• Explosives and Arson
• About ATF	• Laboratories
• Alcohol	• Most Wanted
• Tobacco	• ATF News

Lots of interesting law enforcement information that appears nowhere else.

LAW ENFORCEMENT

Central Intelligence Agency Home Page			
Central Intelligence Agency			
http://www.odci.gov/cia			
GRAPHICS	LINKS	NEWSLETTER	LAWS/REGS
◆	◆		

Includes:
- What's New
- About the CIA

- Publications
- Public Affairs
- Links to Other Intelligence Agency Sites

Incredible source of intelligence information on subjects you might not expect to find on the Internet.

Federal Bureau of Investigation Home Page			
Federal Bureau of Investigation (FBI)			
http://www.fbi.gov/			
GRAPHICS	LINKS	NEWSLETTER	LAWS/REGS
◆	◆		

Includes:
- Subject Index
- Field Offices
- Crime Alert
- Major Investigations
- FBI Academy
- Overview
- Frequently Asked Questions

- FBI's Most Wanted
- What's New
- Press Releases
- Congressional Affairs
- History
- FBI Case Files
- Programs
- Publications

Definitely a first stop for information on law enforcement.

LAW ENFORCEMENT

Police Associations Links			
Police Officer Research Association of California			
http://ifu.net/~x5047x/assc.htm			
GRAPHICS	LINKS	NEWSLETTER	LAWS/REGS
	◆		

Includes:
Links to law enforcement home pages.

Detective Sergeant Tom Bolling's Links to the World			
Detective Sergeant Tom Bolling			
http://www.murlin.com/~webfx/cops/links.html			
GRAPHICS	LINKS	NEWSLETTER	LAWS/REGS
◆	◆		

Includes:
- Police sites and e-mail addresses
- Police Services
- Graphics

This site takes you to almost every major law enforcement link for local law enforcement. Very well organized. It also ties to search engines.

LAW ENFORCEMENT

State Police Agencies (links)			
Lt. Fran Hart, Burlington Police Department			
http://www.bpd.org/state.htm			
GRAPHICS	LINKS	NEWSLETTER	LAWS/REGS
	♦		

Includes:
A listing of a number of state police office home pages.

National Sheriff's Association (NSA) Home Page			
National Sheriff's Association (NSA)			
http://www.sheriffs.org/joinnsa.html			
GRAPHICS	LINKS	NEWSLETTER	LAWS/REGS
	♦	♦	

Includes:
- Membership Division
- Corporate Membership
- National Sheriff's Institute (NSI)
- Community Watch Programs
- Jail Operations
- Sheriff Magazine
- Legislative Monitoring
- Conferences and Conventions
- Crime Prevention Programs
- Research and Development
- Publications

A valued site for Sheriffs and law enforcement interests in general.

LAW ENFORCEMENT

Center for the Study of Intelligence Home Page			
Center for the Study of Intelligence			
http://www.odci.gov/csi			
GRAPHICS	LINKS	NEWSLETTER	LAWS/REGS
		♦	

Includes:
- What's New
- Publications
- Items of Interest

Supports research and publishing on the intelligence profession and its various disciplines, and declassifies historical records related to U.S. intelligence operations during the Cold War.

LAWS/REGULATIONS

Thomas (Jefferson) WWW system of access to current bills, Congressional Record, and bill status			
U.S. Library of Congress			
http://thomas.loc.gov			
GRAPHICS	LINKS	NEWSLETTER	LAWS/REGS
♦	♦		♦

Includes:
- Congress This Week
- Bills
- Laws
- Legislative Process
- Congressional Record
- Committee Information
- Historical Documents
- U.S. Government Links: Legislative, Judicial, State/Local

A powerful site. Every planner should have access to, understand, and use this site.

LAWS/REGULATIONS

Counterpoint Publishing Home Page			
Counterpoint Publishing			
http://www.counterpoint.com/			
GRAPHICS	LINKS	NEWSLETTER	LAWS/REGS
	◆		

Includes:
- Daily Federal Register and Archives
- Current Code of Federal Regulations
- Advanced Technology
- Commerce Business Daily
- Texas Register
- State Environmental/Safety Regulations
- CHEMTOX Internet
- VNR Comprehensive Chemical Contaminant Series
- Government Contract Advisor
- Nuclear Information Service

This is an important vendor site for finding critical and up-to-date laws and regulations. Every emergency manager should seek to get access to these services.

Code of Federal Regulations Internet Law Library			
National Archives and Records Administration			
http://www.access.gpo.gov/nara/cfr/cfr-table-search.html			
GRAPHICS	LINKS	NEWSLETTER	LAWS/REGS
	◆		◆

Includes:
- About CFR Service
- Search the Books by Key Words
- Retrieve Available CFR Sections by Citation
- Search Your Choice of CFR Books

This site provides a comprehensive method to search the current Code of Federal Regulations.

LAWS/REGULATIONS

Find Law Home Page			
Find Law			
http://www.findlaw.com/			
GRAPHICS	LINKS	NEWSLETTER	LAWS/REGS
	◆		◆

Includes:
- Search Engine
- Legal Subject Index
- Law Schools
- Legal Associations
- Law Firms and Lawyers
- Consultants and Experts
- Professional Development
- Laws: Cases and Codes
- U.S. Federal Government Resources
- State Law Resources
- Foreign and International Resources
- News and Reference Materials
- Legal Practice Information

A site to find just about any law and legal quote imaginable. An incredible search engine. Every planner needs this one on their desktop.

Federal Energy Regulatory Commission legal reference section			
Federal Energy Regulatory Commission (FERC)			
http://www.powerquote.com/ferc/fercindex.html			
GRAPHICS	LINKS	NEWSLETTER	LAWS/REGS
			◆

Includes:
Code of Federal Regulations in HTML format that relate to dam operations.

LAWS/REGULATIONS

West Group Home Page			
West Group (home of West Publishing)			
http://www.westlaw.com/			
GRAPHICS	LINKS	NEWSLETTER	LAWS/REGS
			◆

Includes:
- News and Corporate Information
- Legal Practice and Research Products
- Legal Education Products
- Web Services
- West's Legal Director
- Support and Training

The premier Internet location to search for laws and regulations. This is a vendor site.

LIGHTNING

Alden Electronics Home Page			
Alden Lightning Products			
http://alden.com/light1.html			
GRAPHICS	LINKS	NEWSLETTER	LAWS/REGS
◆	◆		

Includes:
- Weather
- Images
- Links
- Information
- Index
- News

A source for the weekly USA lightning map. Wonderful place to visit. Great place to link to other useful sites.

LIGHTNING

National Lightning Safety Institute (NLSI) Home Page			
National Lightning Safety Institute			
http://www.lightningsafety.com			
GRAPHICS	LINKS	NEWSLETTER	LAWS/REGS
◆	◆		

Includes:
- Introduction to NLSI
- NLSI Skills and Services
- The Lightning Safety Problem
- Lightning Losses in the USA
- Personal Lightning Safety
- The Effect of Lightning
- Lightning Safety for Structures
- References and Other Information

A tremendous resource for emergency management planning for lightning.

MAPS

U.S. Geological Survey National Mapping Information			
U.S. Geological Survey			
http://mapping.usgs.gov			
GRAPHICS	LINKS	NEWSLETTER	LAWS/REGS
◆	◆		

Includes:
- News
- Mapping Products and Services
- Browse the Solar System
- National Mapping Program
- Geospatial Data Standards
- Educational Sources
- Regional Mapping Centers
- Links to Other Sites

Topographical maps of the United States.

MITIGATION

Federal Emergency Management Agency (FEMA) Mitigation Directorate			
Federal Emergency Management Agency (FEMA)			
http://www.fema.gov/mit/			
GRAPHICS	LINKS	NEWSLETTER	LAWS/REGS

Includes:
- About Mitigation
- What's New in Mitigation
- Mitigation News Desk
- Mitigation Room FEMA Library
- Mitigation at Work
- Meetings, Conferences, Seminars
- Know Your Risks
- FEMA Map Service Center
- Search Engine

Every U.S. emergency manager should visit this site regularly.

International Center for Disaster Mitigation Engineering (INCEDE)			
University of Tokyo			
http://incede.iis.u-tokyo.ac.jp/Incede.html			
GRAPHICS	LINKS	NEWSLETTER	LAWS/REGS
	♦		

Includes:
- Publications
- Disaster Investigations
- Network
- Kobenet--for the Kobe Earthquake
- Joint Research
- Disaster Information
- Symposia
- INCEDE Activities
- Special Graphics Interface

Focuses on documents about mitigation for flood, earthquake and other natural disasters.

MITIGATION

International Conference of Building Officials (ICBO) Home Page
Custom Standards Services, Inc.
http://www.cssinfo.com/info/icbo.html

GRAPHICS	LINKS	NEWSLETTER	LAWS/REGS

Includes:
- Search Engine
- News Releases
- Links to Other Web Sites
- Catalog Request
- Updating Service

This is a critical site for getting information and perspective on the Uniform Building Code when planning for mitigation activities.

Conference Site: Practical Solutions to Protect Cities at Risk
IDNDR Secretariat and the Pan American Health Organization
http://www.quipu.net

GRAPHICS	LINKS	NEWSLETTER	LAWS/REGS

Includes:
- Education
- Information
- Aid Peru

This site features a running conference on the protection of cities at risk . Information at this site is in English, Spanish and Portuguese.

MITIGATION

Johnstone Centre of Parks, Recreation and Heritage Home Page
Johnstone Centre of Parks, Recreation and Heritage(Charles Stuart University)
http://life.csu.edu.au/~dspennem/MTWILLS/CICRIT.HTM

GRAPHICS	LINKS	NEWSLETTER	LAWS/REGS
	◆		

Includes:
- What's New
- Publications
- Links to Related Sites

A special interest network for natural hazard mitigation for cultural heritage sites.

National Drought Mitigation Center (NDMC) Home Page
University of Nebraska-Lincoln
http://enso.unl.edu/ndmc/index.html

GRAPHICS	LINKS	NEWSLETTER	LAWS/REGS
	◆		

Includes:
- About NDMC
- What's New
- Drought Watch
- Drought Climatology
- Why Plan for Drought
- Mitigating the Effects of Drought
- Drought Planner's Handbook
- Directory of Drought Contacts
- Other Related Links

A one-stop shopping for drought emergency planning and mitigation.

MITIGATION

USGS Response to an Urban Earthquake--Northridge '94: Assisting Recovery, Reconstruction, and Mitigation

U.S. Geological Survey

http://geohazards.cr.usgs.gov/northridge/assist.htm

GRAPHICS	LINKS	NEWSLETTER	LAWS/REGS
♦			

Includes:		
• Summary of Activities	• Table of Contents	
• Main Shock	• Geological Hazards	
	• Links to USGS home page	

A good overview of what government can and should do in response to catastrophic quakes.

Earthquake Mitigation Activities Elsewhere

Oregon Governor's Task Force on the Seismic Rehabilitation of Existing Structures

http://sarvis.dogami.state.or.us/SeRTaF/EQmitigation.htm

GRAPHICS	LINKS	NEWSLETTER	LAWS/REGS

Includes:

Findings of a task force in Oregon involved with potential legislation.

MITIGATION

Earthquake Hazards Mitigation Information Network (EQNET)				
National Center for Earthquake Engineering Research (NCEER)				
Earthquake Hazards Mitigation Center				
http://www.eqnet.org				
GRAPHICS	LINKS	NEWSLETTER	LAWS/REGS
◆	◆		
Includes: • Alphabetic Listing of Information Sources • Information Sources by Subject		• Bibliographic Resources • Images • About EQNET	
A compilation of Internet resource about quake hazards.				

Hurricane Mitigation Strategy for North Florida				
University of Florida				
http://www.co.alachua.fl.us/~acem/htmp.html				
GRAPHICS	LINKS	NEWSLETTER	LAWS/REGS
	◆		
Includes: • Project Summary • Research Overview		• Tools for Windstorm Mitigation • Project Updates • Link to Other Sites	
Home of the Hazard Tree Management Program.				

MITIGATION

International Multi-Hazard Mitigation Partnership Home Page				
International Multi-Hazard Mitigation Partnership			
http://www.inel.gov/capabilities/acets/nmhmp/brochure.html			
GRAPHICS	LINKS	NEWSLETTER	LAWS/REGS
◆			

Includes:
- Disaster Risk Profiles (and map)
- Concept of Operation
- Partners
- Pictures of Major Structural Damage

- Wind Tunnel Testing in Colorado
- The Oklahoma City Bombing
- Links to the Advanced Combined Environments Test Station (ACETS)

This site explains in great detail the partnership's visions and plans to improve mitigation efforts. It is built as an explanatory brochure, and makes an excellent talking paper.

Operation Fresh Start				
Department of Energy			
http://www.sustainable.doe.gov/freshstart/			
GRAPHICS	LINKS	NEWSLETTER	LAWS/REGS
	◆		

Includes:
- About the Operation
- Sustainable Development Overview
- Community Planning
- Recovery Assistance Programs

- Business Recovery
- Rebuilding Your Home
- Emergency Power Sources
- Case Studies
- Links to Other Sites

This is a critical site for finding the latest on federal efforts to improve survivability of communities after disaster.

MITIGATION

Volcanic Hazards Mitigation			
Michigan Technological University			
http://www.geo.mtu.edu/volcanoes/hazards.html			
GRAPHICS	LINKS	NEWSLETTER	LAWS/REGS
◆			

Includes:
- A Basic Guide to Volcanic Hazards
- Santa Maria Volcano
- Cerro Quemado Volcano
- Fuego Volcano
- Tascana Volcano
- Vesuvio Volcano, Italy
- Pinatubo Volcano
- MTU Volcanoes Page Link

A guide to pictures of major active volcanoes around the world.

MUTUAL AID

Mutual Aid: A Factor of Evolution			
Dana Ward, Political Studies Professor - Pitzer College			
http://www.pitzer.edu/~dward/Anarchist_Archives/kropotkin/mutaidcontents.html			
GRAPHICS	LINKS	NEWSLETTER	LAWS/REGS

Includes:
- Mutual Aid Among Animals
- Mutual Aid Among Savages
- Mutual Aid Among Barbarians
- Mutual Aid in the Mediaeval City
- Mutual Aid Amongst Ourselves
- Conclusion
- Appendix

An interesting history of mutual aid through the ages.

MUTUAL AID

Mutual Aid Association of Private School Personnel			
Japan External Trade Organization			
http://www.jetro.go.jp/gov/entity/entity231.html			
GRAPHICS	LINKS	NEWSLETTER	LAWS/REGS
Includes: This is an example of how key personnel in a mutual aid system can be tracked via the Internet.			

NUCLEAR

Nuclear Energy Institute (NEI) Home Page			
Nuclear Energy Institute (NEI)			
http://www.nei.org			
GRAPHICS	LINKS	NEWSLETTER	LAWS/REGS
Includes: • Basics • Benefits	• Atoms at Work • Keeping It Safe • Press Room		
NEI offers a broad spectrum of information about the nuclear power industry, including emergency information. This site offers basic information and educational input on nuclear power.			

NUCLEAR

Nuclear Regulatory Commission (NRC) Home Page			
Nuclear Regulatory Commission (NRC)			
http://www.nrc.gov/			
GRAPHICS	LINKS	NEWSLETTER	LAWS/REGS
◆	◆		

Includes:
- Nuclear Reactors
- Nuclear Materials
- Radioactive Wastes
- News and Information
- Public Involvement with NRC

This is the place to stop first for information on the nuclear power plants in the U.S.

PREPAREDNESS

State and Local Guide for All Hazard Emergency Operations Planning			
Federal Emergency Management Agency (FEMA)			
http://www.fema.gov/pte/gaheop.htm			
GRAPHICS	LINKS	NEWSLETTER	LAWS/REGS
			◆

Includes:
- Preliminary Considerations
- Planning Process
- Emergency Operations Plan Format
- Basic Plan Content
- Functional Annex Content
- Hazard-Unique Planning Considerations
- Linking Federal and State Emergency Response Operations
- Glossary, Acronyms, Bibliography

This document replaces several other key emergency management planning guides, such as CPG 1-8A. A critical document for all U.S. emergency managers.

PREPAREDNESS

Western New York Disaster Preparedness and Recovery Manual for Libraries and Archives			
Western New York Library Council			
http://www.wnylrc.org/pub/disman.htm			
GRAPHICS	LINKS	NEWSLETTER	LAWS/REGS

Includes:
- Introduction
- Worksheet Section
- Reference Section
- Appendix
- Supplier Directory

Every community has a library, and every emergency manager should share this site with their local librarian.

Canadian Centre For Emergency Preparedness Home Page			
Canadian Centre for Emergency Preparedness (CCEP)			
http://alpha.netaccess.on.ca/ccep/			
GRAPHICS	LINKS	NEWSLETTER	LAWS/REGS
	◆		

Includes:
- Conferences
- Training
- Community Emergency Planning Services
- Links to Related Sites

Focuses on providing training for emergency preparedness professionals.

PREPAREDNESS

"How To" Fact Sheets for Disaster Preparedness			
Federal Emergency Management Agency (FEMA)			
http://www.fema.gov/home/fema/prepfact.html			
GRAPHICS	LINKS	NEWSLETTER	LAWS/REGS

Includes:
- Family Disaster Plan
- Home Hazard Hunt
- Disaster Preparedness for People with Disabilities
- Assisting People with Disabilities in a Disaster
- Disaster Supplies Kit
- Pets and Disasters

Just the best fact sheets out on the street for quick explanations of key issues.

Report: Natural Disaster Reduction: A Plan for the Nation			
Subcommittee on Natural Disaster Reduction (SNDR) of the Committee on Environment and Natural Resources, National Science and Technology Council			
http://www.usgs.gov/sndr/report			
GRAPHICS	LINKS	NEWSLETTER	LAWS/REGS

Includes:
- Purpose of the Report
- Committee on Environment and Natural Disasters
- Subcommittee on Natural Disaster Reduction
- Executive Summary
- Strategic Plan

This report should help set long-term strategic goals for U.S. emergency managers.

PREPAREDNESS

University of Illinois Cooperative Extension Service Disaster Services Page
University of Illinois
http://www.ag.uiuc.edu/~disaster/disaster.html

GRAPHICS	LINKS	NEWSLETTER	LAWS/REGS
	◆		

Includes:
- CES Disaster Guide
- Information Resources for Preparedness, Recovery, and Relief
- Agencies
- Organizations
- Severe Weather Warnings

Straightforward. Easy to use. Sends reader through links to the standard fare—with a nice focus on the needs of the general public in public assistance areas. An excellence resource reference for preparedness and planning.

Asian Disaster Preparedness Center
Asian Institute of Technology, Bangkok
http://www.adpc.ait.ac.th/Default.html

GRAPHICS	LINKS	NEWSLETTER	LAWS/REGS
	◆		

Includes:
- Information and Research
- Learning and Professional Development
- Links to Related Sites
- Asian Urban Disaster Mitigation Program International Consultancies and Alumni
- ADPC Disaster Network

Set up since 1986 to help countries in the Asia and Pacific Rim to form policies and strengthen their ability to respond and recover from disaster.

PREPAREDNESS

Emergency Preparedness Information Exchange (EPIX)
Center for Public Policy Research on Science and Technology, Simon Fraser University, Vancouver, B.C.
http://hoshi.cic.sfu.ca/~anderson/

GRAPHICS	LINKS	NEWSLETTER	LAWS/REGS
◆	◆		

Includes:
- About EPIX
- Topic Areas (covers everything)
- Organizations
- Alerts
- Impacts

Great tie to other sites. Wonderful news features. Very fast site. Alert category very valuable for updates on latest events. Definitely a key research site.

Natural Hazards
Emergency Preparedness Canada
http://nais.ccm.emr.ca/~kramers/hazardnet/a_contents/content.htm

GRAPHICS	LINKS	NEWSLETTER	LAWS/REGS
◆	◆		

Includes:
- Earthquakes
- Volcanoes
- Tsunamis
- Winds
- Tornadoes and Hurricanes
- Hail
- Floods/Ocean Danger
- Landslides and Avalanches
- Poster Maps

Wonderful layout. Great site. Tons of information. Nice graphical resource.

PREPAREDNESS

Emergency Preparedness Canada Web Site (English and French version)			
Government of Canada			
http://hoshi.cic.sfu.ca/~epc/			
GRAPHICS	LINKS	NEWSLETTER	LAWS/REGS
	◆	◆	

Includes:	• Information Materials
• On-line magazine (*Emergency Preparedness Digest*)	• Canadian Emergency Preparedness College

RECOVERY

Updates on Planning for Disaster Recovery			
International City/County Management Association (ICMA)			
http://www.icma.org/whatsnew/index.htm			
GRAPHICS	LINKS	NEWSLETTER	LAWS/REGS
	◆		

Includes:	• New Matrix of Recovery Needs
• Bibliography	• Links to Related Sites

Excellent materials on community recovery after a disaster.

RECOVERY

U.S. Social Security Administration Home Page			
U.S. Social Security Administration			
http://www.ssa.gov			
GRAPHICS	LINKS	NEWSLETTER	LAWS/REGS
	◆		◆

Includes:
- Benefits Publications/Information
- Facts and Figures
- Freedom of Information
- International Issues
- Medicare Information
- Public Information Resources
- Laws and Regulations

Good source for information like the number of SS applicants in a county. Also, the income in counties/states by source. Of value for recovery applications.

U.S. Dept. of Veterans Affairs Home Page			
U.S. Department of Veterans Affairs			
http://www.va.gov			
GRAPHICS	LINKS	NEWSLETTER	LAWS/REGS
	◆		

Includes:
- What's New
- Benefits
- Facilities
- Search Engine
- Special Programs
- Organization
- Data
- Medical
- Links to Related Sites

Key site for getting recovery information relevant to vets in a community. Huge databases available in Excel format. Good site.

RECOVERY

Toolkit for Crisis Prevention, Mitigation and Recovery in Africa (CPMR)			
USAID Health and Human Resource Analysis for Africa Project			
http://www.tulane.edu/~inhl/cpmr.htm			
GRAPHICS	LINKS	NEWSLETTER	LAWS/REGS
	♦		

Includes:	• Public Health Crisis Prevention, Mitigation, and Recovery: Linking Relief and Development
• Project Description • Links to Related Sites	

This site has a philosophy that relief and disaster planning are linked to sustainable development.

RELIEF

Mass Relocation Project Home Page			
Landark Foundation			
http://www.webspawner.com/users/landark/			
GRAPHICS	LINKS	NEWSLETTER	LAWS/REGS

Only text, but describes a new concept in preparing fixed facilities for mass care and shelter following the catastrophic loss of a U.S. city. Interesting concept worth considering for relief planning.

RELIEF

International Committee of the Red Cross (ICRC) Home Page, Geneva Switzerland			
International Committee of the Red Cross (ICRC)			
http://www.icrc.ch			
GRAPHICS	LINKS	NEWSLETTER	LAWS/REGS
♦	♦		

Includes:
- What's New
- Photo Album
- Search Engine
- Site Tree
- Links to Other Sites

A critical site for staying aware of relief operations around the world, and approaches to large relief operations. This site features a photo gallery.

Humanitarian Scenarios Home Page			
Aldo and Jan Benini			
http://www.slonet.org/~abenini/			
GRAPHICS	LINKS	NEWSLETTER	LAWS/REGS
	♦		

Includes:
- Computer Simulation of Humanitarian Scenarios
- Simulating the Effectiveness of Humanitarian Action
- Ebola Strikes the Global Village
- Uncertainty and Information Flows in Humanitarian Agencies
- Early Warning Systems for Violent Conflict
- Relief Economics: Walking in a Political Minefield

A simply wonderful site showing what a difference just two people in emergency management can do to improve world conditions.

RELIEF

International Emergency and Refugee Health Program site, associated with the Refugee Health Program			
U.S. Department of Health and Human Services			
http://www.cdc.gov/nceh/programs/internat/ierh/ierh.htm			
GRAPHICS	LINKS	NEWSLETTER	LAWS/REGS
♦	♦		

Includes:
- Program Descriptions
- What's New
- CDC Publications and Recommendations
- Sites and Related Information

Provides lots of information on the topic, many links, and is very easy to use. Also has numerous photos, some not for the weak of heart.

Relief Now Web Site			
Faith based non-profits doing humanitarian work			
http://www.villagelife.org/satellite/reliefnow.html			
GRAPHICS	LINKS	NEWSLETTER	LAWS/REGS
♦	♦		

Includes:
- Children Needs
- Relief Supplies Currently Needed
- Disaster Updates
- How to Donate/Volunteer
- Links to Other Sites

Central site for information on humanitarian aid efforts. Great place to find out what VOAD-type organizations are doing. One of best information sites for total costs and efforts I've seen on the Web, and one of the most up-to-date, based on the most recent efforts. Very valuable to all levels of planning.

RELIEF

Relief Web			
UN Department of Humanitarian Affairs (DHA)			
http://www.reliefweb.int			
GRAPHICS	LINKS	NEWSLETTER	LAWS/REGS
◆	◆		

Includes:
- Emergencies
- Bulletins
- Resources
- Map Center
- Financial Tracking
- Search Engine
- DHA-Online

This site consolidates and organizes information produced by a wide range of sources on current humanitarian crises/natural disasters worldwide. It features a full library and tons of maps. Also, a very up-to-date listing of current world disasters.

National Emergency Resource Information Network (NERIN) Home Page			
National Emergency Resource Information Network (NERIN)			
http://www.cdd.sc.edu/4nerin/			
GRAPHICS	LINKS	NEWSLETTER	LAWS/REGS
	◆		

Includes:
- Goals
- NERIN Description
- NERIN Accreditation
- Model Components
- Project Partners
- National Resources
- Interactive Model Development

This site features the formation of an incredibly valuable pilot project to coordinate local resources on a national database with real-time Internet access for relief.

RELIEF

The International Society of Logistics (SOLE) Home Page			
The International Society of Logistics (SOLE)			
http://www.sole.org/			
GRAPHICS	LINKS	NEWSLETTER	LAWS/REGS

Includes:
- Information on SOLE
- Career Assistance Program
- Logistics Business Network
- Software Library
- Hot News and Calendar of Events
- Certified Professional Logistician
- Ask the Experts
- LOGtalk
- Links to Other Sites

This site helps address one of the toughest problems facing emergency management today: the movement of resources and their handling to and from a disaster site.

RESEARCH

Natural Hazards Research and Applications Center			
University of Colorado, Boulder			
http://www.colorado.edu/hazards			
GRAPHICS	LINKS	NEWSLETTER	LAWS/REGS
	♦	♦	

Includes:
- Periodicals
- Publications
- Index of Disaster Information
- Disaster Organizations
- Index to Research Institutions
- Directory to Courses of Study
- Upcoming Conferences

One of the key sites for all emergency professionals to visit to gather information. Home of the excellent periodical, *The Natural Hazards Observer*.

RESEARCH

Natural Hazards Research Centre (NHRC)			
Macquarie University, Sydney, Australia			
http://www.es.mq.edu.au/NHRC/			
GRAPHICS	LINKS	NEWSLETTER	LAWS/REGS
	◆	◆	

Includes:
- *Natural Hazards Quarterly*
- Completed Projects
- Publications
- Staff
- Current Projects

Has an on-line newsletter, and some links, but is very focused on Australia's emergency management community.

What's New at the Federal Emergency Management Agency (FEMA)			
Federal Emergency Management Agency (FEMA)			
http://www.fema.gov/fema/whatsnew.htm			
GRAPHICS	LINKS	NEWSLETTER	LAWS/REGS
	◆		

Includes:
- Career Opportunities
- Conferences and Seminars
- FEMA Radio Network
- GEMS: Global Links
- Library
- News Room
- Tropical Storm Watch

The latest information pieces from and about FEMA and disaster operations/recovery.

RESEARCH

National Science Foundation News Service			
National Science Foundation			
http://www.nsf.gov/home/cns/start.htm			
GRAPHICS	LINKS	NEWSLETTER	LAWS/REGS
A custom news service to update reader on new materials and publications.			

Bureau of National Affairs Communications (BNAC) Home Page			
Bureau of National Affairs, Inc.			
http://www.bna.com/bnac/			
GRAPHICS	LINKS	NEWSLETTER	LAWS/REGS
Includes: • What's New • Human Resources Training Programs		• Safety Training Programs • About BNAC • Search Engine	
This is a vendor site for worldwide news for legal, business, tax, labor, health and safety fields. This part of the Bureau of National Affairs, Inc. is involved with providing training solutions, some of which have a bearing on some emergency management issues.			

RESEARCH

GALENET			
Gale Research			
http://www.gale.com/gale.html			
GRAPHICS	LINKS	NEWSLETTER	LAWS/REGS
	◆		

Includes:
- What's New
- Product Catalog
- Press Room
- GALENET
- Resource Center

Cyberhound Online search site for getting assistance in finding information on the Internet. A great site to learn how to find things on the Internet from an advanced perspective.

U.S. Government Accounting Office (GAO) Home Page			
U.S. Government Accounting Office (GAO)			
http://www.gao.gov			
GRAPHICS	LINKS	NEWSLETTER	LAWS/REGS
			◆

Includes:
- GAO Reports and Testimonies
- Comptroller General Decisions and Opinions
- Reports on Federal Agency Major Rules
- GAO Policy and Guidance Materials
- Special Publications and Software
- GAO FraudNET
- About GAO
- What's New

The U.S. General Accounting Office has a tremendous repository of records and reports relevant to almost every aspect of emergency management.

RESEARCH

Government Institutes, Inc. Home Page			
Government Institutes, Inc.			
http://www.govinst.com/			
GRAPHICS	LINKS	NEWSLETTER	LAWS/REGS

Includes:
- What's New/What's Hot
- Educational Courses and Seminars
- Publications
- Customer Service
- About Government Institutes

A great source for environment, health, safety and telecommunications information, Internet guides, and the Code of Federal Regulations; lots of great training course offerings.

General Accounting Office (GAO) Comptroller General Decisions Online			
U.S. Government Printing Office and General Accounting Office			
http://www.access.gpo.gov/su_docs/aces/aces170.shtml			
GRAPHICS	LINKS	NEWSLETTER	LAWS/REGS
	◆		

Includes:
- Helpful Hints
- List of Databases
- Search Engine

GPO WAIS database for finding Comptroller General decisions.

RESEARCH

General Accounting Office (GAO) Reports Online			
U.S. Government Printing Office and General Accounting Office			
http://www.access.gpo.gov/su_docs/aces/aces160.shtml			
GRAPHICS	LINKS	NEWSLETTER	LAWS/REGS
Includes:		• List of Databases	
• Helpful Hints		• Search Engine	
GPO WAIS database for finding reports and testimony.			

Government Information Locator Service (GILS)			
GPO Access			
http://www.access.gpo.gov/su_docs/gils/gils.html			
GRAPHICS	LINKS	NEWSLETTER	LAWS/REGS
Includes:		• Browser Pathways	
• What is GILS		• Browser Pointers	
• Hints		• Final Report on GILS	
This is a sophisticated method used to identify, locate, and describe publicly available Federal information resources, including electronic information resources. You can find public information resources within the Federal Government, and a description of the information available in these resources; you can then use the system to assist in obtaining the information.			

RESEARCH

Library of Congress Home Page			
Library of Congress			
http://www.loc.gov			
GRAPHICS	LINKS	NEWSLETTER	LAWS/REGS
	♦		

Includes:
- Site Search Engine
- Catalog Search Engine
- What's New
- Special Programs

- General Information
- Thomas Legislative Information
- Library Services
- Research Tools
- Links to U.S. Copyright Office

Simply one of the most critical and important sources of information in the world. If it was printed in the last 100 years, copyrighted, or patented, you will find it here.

National Academy Press Home Page			
Publishers for the National Academy of Sciences, National Academy of Engineering, National Institutes of Medicine, National Research Council			
http://www.nap.edu			
GRAPHICS	LINKS	NEWSLETTER	LAWS/REGS
♦	♦		

Includes:
- Welcome Center
- Bookstore

- Reading Room
- Fresh Paint (What's New)
- Press Releases

If you ever wanted to find the latest and the hottest subject areas. A planning researcher's dream.

RESEARCH

Research-It Home Page			
iTools			
http://www.itools.com/research-it/research-it.html			
GRAPHICS	LINKS	NEWSLETTER	LAWS/REGS
	♦		

Includes:
- Language Tools (including translation)
- Library Tools
- Geographical Tools
- Financial Tools
- Shipping and Mailing Tools
- Internet Search Engine Tools
- LISTSERV Search Engine

A very specialized research tool for the most advanced research needs. This requires some effort to fully utilize, due to the huge number of quality tools that are offered. The e-mail listserv search engine is superb.

Why Files of the National Institute for Science Education: explains things in easily understandable terms			
University of Wisconsin and National Science Foundation			
http://whyfiles.news.wisc.edu/			
GRAPHICS	LINKS	NEWSLETTER	LAWS/REGS
♦			

Includes:
- Science Images
- Sports
- Why Files (Archives)
- Forum
- About Why Files

This is a great way for emergency managers to look up a quick explanation for science issues that may come up during emergency management presentations.

RESEARCH

International Journal of Mass Emergencies and Disasters Home Page			
International Sociological Association's Research Committee on Disasters			
http://www.usc.edu/dept/puad/ijmed			
GRAPHICS	LINKS	NEWSLETTER	LAWS/REGS

Includes:	
• About the Journal	• How to Submit Articles
• Contents of Recent Issues	• Editorial Board Members
• Upcoming Articles, Books, Reviews	• Subscriptions

A site for finding out about some of the cutting-edge disaster research.

Global Change Master Directory (GMCD) of earth sciences data			
NASA, Goddard Space Flight Center			
http://gcmd.gsfc.nasa.gov			
GRAPHICS	LINKS	NEWSLETTER	LAWS/REGS
	◆		

Includes:	
• Controlled Search	• Master Directory Field
• Earth Science Links	• Software/Documents
• Announcements	• Projects/Outreach
	• Forum

The Global Change Master Directory (GCMD) is a comprehensive source of information about Earth science, environmental, biosphere, climate, and global change data. This is a superior site for research.

RESEARCH

US Fire Administration Learning Resource Center (LRC) Online Card Catalog
Federal Emergency Management Agency (FEMA)
http://www.lrc.fema.gov

GRAPHICS	LINKS	NEWSLETTER	LAWS/REGS
			◆

Includes:
* Inter-library Loan
* Search Engine

This index provides access to the National Emergency Training Center (NETC) Learning Resource Center. Allows text to be sent on inter-library loan. Allows search by years and format of document, like report, book, CD, etc.

RISK MANAGEMENT

Riskworld
WWW publication on risk assessment and risk management
http://www.riskworld.com

GRAPHICS	LINKS	NEWSLETTER	LAWS/REGS
	◆	◆	

Includes:
* Front Page (news reports/articles)
* New Books
* Abstracts Library
* Software
* Organization
* Links to Related Sites
* Calendar of Events
* Courses/Workshops
* Newsgroups

Provides the latest news about risk management and risk assessment.

RISK MANAGEMENT

The Society for Risk Analysis (SRA) Home Page			
The Society for Risk Analysis			
http://www.sra.org			
GRAPHICS	LINKS	NEWSLETTER	LAWS/REGS
	◆		

Includes:
- About SRA, Membership, Chapters
- Events
- News
- Risk Science
- Links to Related Sites

SATELLITE INFORMATION

Satellite Data			
The Living Earth Inc.			
http://www.fourmilab.ch/cgi-bin/uncgi/Earth/action?opt=-p			
GRAPHICS	LINKS	NEWSLETTER	LAWS/REGS
◆	◆		

Includes:
A variety of fantastic satellite views taken from various perspectives above the Earth.

This site provides a tremendous variety of earth images from space: day, night, latitude, longitude, weather, etc.

SATELLITE INFORMATION

Earth Observation for Identification of Natural Disasters (EOFIND) Center of Earth Observation (CEO) Newsletter of the European Commission			
European Commission			
http://www.ceo.org/april97.html			
GRAPHICS	LINKS	NEWSLETTER	LAWS/REGS
	◆		
Includes: Linkage to papers on the use of satellite technology to prepare for, respond to, and recover from and mitigate disasters.			
New ideas, with some far reaching potential to reduce the costs of future disasters.			

The IDRISI Project			
Clark University Labs for Cartographic Technology and Geographic Analysis			
http://www.idrisi.clarku.edu/			
GRAPHICS	LINKS	NEWSLETTER	LAWS/REGS
	◆		
Includes: • Information • News	• Links to Related Sites • Resource Center • Research		
The purpose of this project is to further the development and understanding of computer-assisted geographic analysis (GIS) processes in disaster operations. This site has case studies, links, and bibliographies.			

SEARCH AND RESCUE

SAR [Search and Rescue] Contacts Page			
Blue Ridge Mountain Rescue Group			
http://www.virginia.edu/~brmrg/sar_contacts			
GRAPHICS	LINKS	NEWSLETTER	LAWS/REGS
◆	◆		

Includes:
- Canadian SAR Home Page Links
- US Links
- National SAR Link
- International SAR Links
- Special topic areas for : Dive, K-9, Technical, Communications, and Law

Over 100 contacts with other search and rescue groups in the US and other countries.

California Task Force-7 Medical Team's Home Page			
Medical Component of the Sacramento Urban Search and Rescue Task Force			
http://www.mother.com/~hxgarzon/usar.htm			
GRAPHICS	LINKS	NEWSLETTER	LAWS/REGS
◆	◆		

Includes:
- Documents on This Web Site
- Documents on Other Web Site
- Links to Related Sites

Great site: many links, good information, good photos.

SEARCH AND RESCUE

National Institute of Urban Search and Rescue Home Page				
National Institute of Urban Search and Rescue (NI/USR)				
http://emergencyservices.com/niusr/				
GRAPHICS	LINKS	NEWSLETTER	LAWS/REGS
◆	◆	◆	

Includes:
- About NI/USR
- Hot Items and Links
- Programs
- Conferences and Events
- Research/Technology
- Articles
- XII Project
- Vision 2000
- People

This site is extremely user friendly and includes the newsletter *Press On.*

SPACE SCIENCE

National Aeronautics and Space Administration (NASA) Home Page.				
National Aeronautics and Space Administration (NASA)				
http://www.nasa.gov				
GRAPHICS	LINKS	NEWSLETTER	LAWS/REGS
◆	◆		

Includes:
- News
- NASA Centers
- Space Science
- Mission to Planet Earth
- Gallery of Video, Graphics, Audio Clips
- Aeronautics
- Human Space Flight
- Education

This site has planning uses for disaster scenarios. Everyone ought to have this on their list, no matter what. It's won about every award for a home page that exists.

SPACE SCIENCE

Natural Disaster References Database Home Page			
NASA, Earth Sciences Directorate of NASA Goddard Space Flight Center			
http://ltpwww.gsfc.nasa.gov/ndrd			
GRAPHICS	LINKS	NEWSLETTER	LAWS/REGS
◆	◆		
Includes: • What's New • Database • Research		• Bulletin Board • Other Sites • Images • Search Engines	
Lots of good information, interesting links and photos, and great bulletin board. One of the most improved sites on emergency management. Very user friendly.			

STRESS

Center for Counter-Conditioning Therapy Home Page. Select: Non-cognitive trauma programs			
The Human Services Clinic, Oakland, California			
http://www.slip.net/~ccthera			
GRAPHICS	LINKS	NEWSLETTER	LAWS/REGS
Includes: • Clinical Papers		• Substance Abuse • Non-Cognitive Trauma Programs	
Critical information for examples of problems associated with Post Traumatic Incident Stress, especially after disasters.			

STRESS

Mass Emergencies Project			
Bar-Ilan University, Israel			
http://www.biu.ac.il:80/SOC/sw/emerge.html			
GRAPHICS	LINKS	NEWSLETTER	LAWS/REGS
◆	◆		

Includes:
- Links
- Research References

MEP promotes effective, measured intervention on all levels by mental health and welfare professionals. Special emphasis is on inherent individual capacity to cope with adversity, and community-based planning and management of response to human needs in emergencies.

Sleep Deprivation Studies			
U.S. ARMY: Walter Reed Army Hospital Institute of Research: Ft. Detrick Maryland			
http://wrair-www.army.mil/depts/Neuropsych/behavbio/behavbiohp.htm			
GRAPHICS	LINKS	NEWSLETTER	LAWS/REGS

Includes:
- Sleep, Sleep Deprivation and Human Performance
- Publications
- Points of Contact
- Department Personnel

A must for HR staff and Safety Officers responsible for safety and performance of emergency responders. Excellent combat medical information source.

TERRORISM

Counter -Terrorism Home Page			
Victor Biro			
http://www.terrorism.net/			
GRAPHICS	LINKS	NEWSLETTER	LAWS/REGS
	♦		

Includes:
- Discussion Groups
- Publications
- Links to Related Sites
- Travel Advisories
- Search Engine
- Multimedia Conference Center

One-stop shopping for key counter-terrorism information.

Granite Island Group Technical Surveillance Counter Measures			
James Atkinson, Consultant			
http://www.tscm.com/			
GRAPHICS	LINKS	NEWSLETTER	LAWS/REGS
♦	♦		

Includes:
- FAQ
- Basic and Advanced Topics
- Techniques to Find Bugs
- Computer Security
- Logistical Issues
- Photo Gallery of Bugging
- Reference Library
- Search Engine
- Related Technical Articles

Mostly advertising, but has some very good ideas. Nice to have a private sector contact point for this topic.

TERRORISM

Edgewood Enterprise Home Page			
U.S. Army Chemical and Biological Defense Command at Aberdeen Proving Ground, Maryland			
http://www.cbdcom.apgea.army.mil/RDA/			
GRAPHICS	LINKS	NEWSLETTER	LAWS/REGS
	♦		

Includes:
- Edgewood Research, Development and Engineering Center (ERDEC)
- Biological Defense Systems
- NBC Defense Systems
- Smoke Obscurants

The Edgewood Enterprise is part of the U.S. Army Chemical and Biological Defense Command at Aberdeen Proving Ground, Maryland.

EMI Measurement and Mitigation			
U. S. Naval Undersea Warfare Center (NUWC)			
http://www.ev.hawaii.edu/Information/NAVC/projects/proj7.html			
GRAPHICS	LINKS	NEWSLETTER	LAWS/REGS

Includes:
- Only a description of the project.

This project evaluates the possible use of electromagnetic interference to disable ground vehicles from military aircraft. This may have some bearing in planning for tactical efforts in counter-terrorism.

TERRORISM

Terrorist Group Profiles pages			
Dudley Know Library, U.S. Navy			
http://web.nps.navy.mil/~library/tgp/tgp.htm			
GRAPHICS	LINKS	NEWSLETTER	LAWS/REGS
Includes:			
• Definitions • Patterns of Global Terrorism		• Chronology of Significant Terrorist Incidents: 1193, 94, 95 • Terrorist Group Profiles	
The information contained in this document and its links is taken from the annually produced U.S. Department of State publication, *Patterns of Global Terrorism.*			

TOOLS

Hypertext Webster Dictionary On Line			
Webster Dictionary			
http://c.gp.cs.cmu.edu:5103/prog/webster			
GRAPHICS	LINKS	NEWSLETTER	LAWS/REGS
	◆		
Includes:			
• Search Engine			
Type the word into the search engine and let it work for you. Acts like an synonym tool and links to original uses.			

TOOLS

Bartlett's Quotations			
Bartlett's Quotations			
http://www.columbia.edu/acis/bartleby/bartlett/			
GRAPHICS	LINKS	NEWSLETTER	LAWS/REGS

Includes:
- Bibliographic Record
- Alphabetical Index of All Authors
- A Chronology of the Authors
- Front Matter and Preface
- Project Bartleby

An important writing tool for emergency management, especially for highlights at beginnings of chapters, for slide shows, and for public talks. The chronology of authors is an historical gem.

Roget's Thesaurus			
Roget's Thesaurus			
http://humanities.uchicago.edu/forms_unrest/ROGET.html			
GRAPHICS	LINKS	NEWSLETTER	LAWS/REGS

Includes:
- Search Engines
- Links to Webster's Dictionary

Great, award winning site. Got to have this one for any writing project.

TOOLS

Cybermaps Home Page			
DeLorme Mapping			
http://www.delorme.com/cyberatlas/			
GRAPHICS	LINKS	NEWSLETTER	LAWS/REGS
♦	♦		
Includes:			

- Powerful search engine
- Incredible maps of all U.S. destinations

An incredible site for cybermaps of the United States.

Mapquest Home Page			
GeoSystems Global Corporation			
http://www.mapquest.com/			
GRAPHICS	LINKS	NEWSLETTER	LAWS/REGS
♦	♦		

Includes:

- Find A Place
- Driving Directions
- Personalized Maps
- Map Shortcuts
- New Technology
- ShopQuest
- GeoTrivia

A varied and powerful site for making cybermaps, plotting directions, and finding locations. Very useful for exercises and for emergency response.

TOOLS

National Yellow Pages Site			
Yellow Pages			
http://www.bigyellow.com			
GRAPHICS	LINKS	NEWSLETTER	LAWS/REGS
◆	◆		

Includes:
- Businesses
- People
- E-Mail
- Global Directory
- Directory Store
- Web Search Engine
- Webkit

Critical tool for finding types of resources and their locations. A must to keep on the desk.

Photodisc Home Page			
Photodisc			
http://www.photodisc.com			
GRAPHICS	LINKS	NEWSLETTER	LAWS/REGS
◆		◆	

Includes:
- Image Collection
- Search Engine
- Design Mind
- *In the Loupe* magazine
- License Information

Vendor allows you to get high resolution photos without royalty problems for your presentations.

TOOLS

City Net Home Page			
Excite, Inc.			
http://www.city.net/			
GRAPHICS	LINKS	NEWSLETTER	LAWS/REGS
◆	◆		

Includes:
- Search Engine
- Search by Region (by Map)

- Links to Related Sites
- Ties to Travel Essentials, Ticketmaster, Farefinder

This site is for finding information about cities and counties and countries for travel. As much as we travel in this business, we all better have this on board.

Unit Conversion Site			
Edwards Aquifer Research and Data Center (EARDC)			
http://www.eardc.swt.edu/cgi-bin/ucon/ucon.pl			
GRAPHICS	LINKS	NEWSLETTER	LAWS/REGS

Includes:
- Unit Converter for Almost Any Imaginable Unit of Measure

- Links to Other Sites

Everyone ought to have this quick reference to convert units from one to the other. Great tool.

TOOLS

Zip Code Finder			
U.S. Post Office			
http://www.usps.gov/ncsc/lookups/lookup_ctystzip.html			
GRAPHICS	LINKS	NEWSLETTER	LAWS/REGS

Includes:
- Search Engine
- Stamps
- Rate Calculator
- Change of Address
- ZIP Codes
- Express Mail Tracking
- State Abbreviations

What's more useful than a zip code finder at your fingertips?

Thomas Register Listing of Manufacturers			
Thomas Register			
http://www.thomasregister.com:8000/			
GRAPHICS	LINKS	NEWSLETTER	LAWS/REGS

Includes:
- Search Engine
- Free Membership
- Marketing and Advertising
- Free Demos
- Other Resources

A must for every emergency professional during response and recovery if you work in logistics and need to find critical equipment and vendor services.

TORNADO

Tornado Project Online			
The Tornado Project			
http://www.tornadoproject.com			
GRAPHICS	LINKS	NEWSLETTER	LAWS/REGS
◆	◆		

Includes:
- Recent Tornadoes
- Tornado Project
- Videos and Books
- Past Tornadoes
- Storm Chasing
- Favorite Sites
- Fujita Scale
- All States
- Top Ten Tornadoes
- Oddities, Stories, Myth
- Safety

Superb site for data and research on tornadoes.

TRAINING

California Specialized Training Institute (CSTI) Home Page			
California Governor's Office of Emergency Services			
http://www.csti.org/			
GRAPHICS	LINKS	NEWSLETTER	LAWS/REGS

Includes:
- About the Governor's Office of Emergency Services
- About CSTI
- History of CSTI
- Participant Profile
- Administrative Information
- Maps to CSTI

A simply superb vendor of emergency management training in North America.

TRAINING

Simeon Institute			
Pacific Emergency Management Center (Associated with California OES/CSTI)			
http://www.simeon.org			
GRAPHICS	LINKS	NEWSLETTER	LAWS/REGS
◆	◆		
Includes: • Class Listing		• Extension Services • Links to Useful Documents	
This site is very focused as a vendor of education. It does feature a complete dictionary of emergency preparedness terms: Emergency Services. Also links to the "News Interview Survival Guide", and a Disaster Communications bookshelf.			

Crisis and Emergency Management Master of Science in Management			
Center for the Study of Emergency Management : Hope International University			
http://www.simeon.org/msm.html			
GRAPHICS	LINKS	NEWSLETTER	LAWS/REGS
Includes: • Schedule		• List of Courses • Course Requirements	
A new organization associated with the California Specialized Training Institute.			

TRAINING

University of Wisconsin-Disaster Management Center			
University of Wisconsin, Department of Engineering Professional Development			
http://epdwww.engr.wisc.edu/dmc/			
GRAPHICS	LINKS	NEWSLETTER	LAWS/REGS
	♦		

Includes:
- Course of Study in Emergency Management
- Emergency Settlement Project
- Links to Other Sites

This site offers, through the University, an excellent distance learning opportunity for emergency management professionals.

Independent Study Program			
Federal Emergency Management Agency (FEMA)			
http://www.fema.gov/EMI/ishome.htm			
GRAPHICS	LINKS	NEWSLETTER	LAWS/REGS
	♦		

Includes:
- Course List
- Enrollment Directions
- Connections to FEMA home page

A must for emergency planners. Here's where the beginner can earn background credentials, and the seasoned pro can get a quick refresher of the basics.

TRAINING

Training Class List at Emergency Management Institute (EMI)			
Federal Emergency Management Agency (FEMA)			
http://www.fema.gov/EMI/emi.htm			
GRAPHICS	LINKS	NEWSLETTER	LAWS/REGS

Includes:
- EMI Catalogue of Activities

Here is where to get the FEMA emergency management training courses that prepare all U.S. planners. Still under construction.

TRANSPORTATION

Federal Aviation Administration (FAA) Home Page			
Federal Aviation Administration (FAA)			
http://www.faa.gov/			
GRAPHICS	LINKS	NEWSLETTER	LAWS/REGS
◆	◆		

Includes:
- Hot Topics
- Web Site Map
- Search Engine
- What's New
- DOT home page Link
- Feedback Area
- Quick Jump Tool

A particularly good site to find the latest regulations and safety inquiry information. If there is anything about aviation and airport planning you need, this is the site.

TRANSPORTATION

U.S. Department of Transportation (US DOT) Home Page			
U.S. Department of Transportation (US DOT)			
http://www.dot.gov/			
GRAPHICS	LINKS	NEWSLETTER	LAWS/REGS
♦	♦		♦

Includes:
- What's Hot at DOT
- Contacts
- News and Statistics
- Legislation and Regulations
- National Transportation Library
- Safety Issues
- Links to Related Sites

This is the gateway to a number of other federal agencies that are under the US. DOT. It's a good place to start to look for information on any kind of transportation issues.

U.S. Federal Highway Administration (FHWA) Home Page			
U.S. Federal Highway Administration (FHWA)			
http://cti1.volpe.dot.gov/ohim/			
GRAPHICS	LINKS	NEWSLETTER	LAWS/REGS
♦	♦		

Includes:
- Site Content Index
- What's New
- Organization
- Reports, Products, and Publications
- Data Provider
- Related Links
- Customer Service Contacts

If you have any questions about the interstate highway system and issues about interstate travel, this is the site. May be useful in critical evacuation and logistics movement planning.

TRANSPORTATION

U.S. Coast Guard Home Page			
U.S. Coast Guard			
http://www.dot.gov/dotinfo/uscg/welcome.html			
GRAPHICS	LINKS	NEWSLETTER	LAWS/REGS
◆	◆		

Includes:
- News and Current Events
- Services and Programs
- How to Reach the Coast Guard
- Facts, Images, History
- What's New
- Links to Related Sites

This site is for information on everything from weather to oil spills. A great site, with plenty of useful links.

Federal Railroad Administration (FRA) Home Page			
Federal Railroad Administration (FRA)			
http://www.dot.gov/dotinfo/fra/welcome.html			
GRAPHICS	LINKS	NEWSLETTER	LAWS/REGS
◆	◆		◆

Includes:
- FRA: Who We Are and What We Do
- Mission and Vision
- Office of Safety
- High Speed Ground Transportation
- Doing Business with the FRA
- Office of Public Affairs
- Asian Pacific American Employees Council
- Gage Restraint Measurement System
- Research and Development
- FRA Search Engine
- Link to U.S. DOT home page

This site provides railroad information, including accidents and regulations.

TRANSPORTATION

U.S. Bureau of Transportation Statistics Home Page			
U.S. Department of Transportation			
http://www.bts.gov/			

GRAPHICS	LINKS	NEWSLETTER	LAWS/REGS
◆	◆		◆

Includes:
- What's New
- Briefing Room
- Site Map
- National Transportation Library
- Geographic Information Services
- BTS Programs
- Databases
- BTS Products and Services
- Other Transportation Resources

An incredible source of data and discussions on transportation issues, along with information about regulatory interpretation.

National Transportation Safety Board (NTSB) Home Page			
National Transportation Safety Board (NTSB)			
http://www.ntsb.gov/			

GRAPHICS	LINKS	NEWSLETTER	LAWS/REGS
◆	◆		

Includes:
- Search Engine
- Upcoming Events
- Speeches and Testimony
- Press Releases
- Employment Opportunities
- Aviation Accidents
- Highway Accidents
- Marine Accidents
- Pipeline/Hazardous Materials Accidents
- Railroad Accidents

For current crash information and scenarios of hundreds of other crashes.

TSUNAMI

Tsunami			
University of Washington			
http://www.geophys.washington.edu/tsunami/welcome.html			
GRAPHICS	LINKS	NEWSLETTER	LAWS/REGS
◆	◆		

Includes:
- General Tsunami Information
- Tsunami Survey and Research
- Miscellaneous Information

Very direct, clean design. Lots of good information and photos. Good links. Good historical files. For the serious and general reader. Features some mitigation information.

Journal of the Tsunami Society, *Science of Tsunami Hazards*			
Center of Coastal and Land-Margin Research of the Oregon Graduate Institute of Science & Technology			
http://www.ccalmr.ogi.edu/STH			
GRAPHICS	LINKS	NEWSLETTER	LAWS/REGS
◆	◆		

Includes:
- Current Issue
- All Issues
- Submittal Instructions
- Links to Related Sites
- Announcements

Very focused. Does what it offers. Tsunami links. Designed for the serious researcher, not a casual browser.

TSUNAMI

Science of Tsunami Hazards Home Page			
The Tsunami Society/Center of Coastal and Land-Margin Research of the Oregon Graduate Institute of Science and Technology			
http://www.geophys.washington.edu/tsunami/welcome.html			
GRAPHICS	LINKS	NEWSLETTER	LAWS/REGS
	◆	◆	
Includes: • Current Issue of Journal • All Issues		• Links to Related Sites • Announcements	
This site features the *International Journal of the Tsunami Society*.			

VENDORS

G.D. Barri & Associates Home Page			
G.D. Barri & Associates			
http://www.gdbarri.com/			
GRAPHICS	LINKS	NEWSLETTER	LAWS/REGS
	◆	◆	
Includes: • About G.D. Barri and Associates • Who's Who		• Newsletter • Classified Ads • Links to Related Sites	
A reliable vendor site with lots of valuable resources for every organization.			

VENDORS

Community Alert Network			
Community Alert Network (CAN)			
http://www.can-intl.com/			
GRAPHICS	LINKS	NEWSLETTER	LAWS/REGS
	♦	♦	

Includes:	• Typical Users and FAQ
• General Information	• Request Form
• CAN Toolbox	• CAN Newsletter
• Download Demo	

A critical site for all the managers who already use this superb service to notify the public when there is an impending threat. A must vendor site for disaster preparedness.

Disaster Resource Guide **Magazine Home Page**			
Emergency Lifeline Corporation			
http://www.disaster-resource.com			
GRAPHICS	LINKS	NEWSLETTER	LAWS/REGS
♦	♦		

Includes:	• Bibliography
• Articles	• Organizations
• Products/Services	• Trade Shows
	• Resources

They present this as a one-stop resource for educational, organizational and vendor resources.

VENDORS

Emergency: A Guide to Emergency Services of the World			
Justin Kibell, Melbourne, Australia			
http://www.catt.citri.edu.au/emergency/emergency.html			
GRAPHICS	LINKS	NEWSLETTER	LAWS/REGS
◆	◆		

Includes:
- What's New
- Photo Gallery
- Patch Photos
- Patch Collectors
- Notice Board
- Virtual Emergency
- Training Room
- Links to Other Sites
- Guest Book
- Search Engine
- Visitor Survey

This site offers a guide for emergency services everywhere. Lots of links to other disaster recovery sites. Truly one of the best all-around sites for emergency response personnel on the Web. It has a wonderful photo library. Also great stories about real field response.

Bry-Air, Inc. Home Page			
Bry-Air, Inc.			
http://database.sweets.com:8080/sweets/p1/Company/2062.htm			
GRAPHICS	LINKS	NEWSLETTER	LAWS/REGS
	◆		

Includes:
- Products and Services
- Links to Other Sites

This vendor manufactures desiccant dehumidifiers and environmental control systems for industrial drying applications. A good vendor to have on file for drying out large facilities and offices after flooding.

VENDORS

Document Recovery Systems Home Page			
Drying Systems International, Inc. (DSII)			
http://www.mmedia.com/clients/drying/			
GRAPHICS	LINKS	NEWSLETTER	LAWS/REGS
	◆		
Includes:			
Just a single page offering services.			
A vendor with resources to recover lost and damaged files.			

VOLCANO

Alaska Volcano Observatory			
USGS , University of Alaska Fairbanks Geophysical Institute and the Alaska Division of Geological and Geophysical Surveys			
http://www.avo.alaska.edu			
GRAPHICS	LINKS	NEWSLETTER	LAWS/REGS
◆	◆		
Includes:			
• Updates • Other Volcanoes			
• General Information • Inside AVO			
• Monitored Volcanoes • Resources			
• Links to Related Sites			
Well designed. One of the easier sites for finding quality information quickly. Very colorful. Lots of great photos. Great links to other sites. A fun, and educational site to visit. Very useful chronological files on Alaska volcano sites.			

VOLCANO

Cascade Volcano Observatory			
U. S. Department of the Interior			
http://vulcan.wr.usgs.gov/home.html			
GRAPHICS	LINKS	NEWSLETTER	LAWS/REGS
◆	◆		

Includes:
- Updates
- General Information
- Monitored Volcanoes
- Other Volcanoes
- Resources

Nice site. Simple layout. This is the place for volcano lovers. Great photos. Specific research section with explanation, graphics, maps, references.

Volcano World			
University of North Dakota			
http://volcano.und.edu/			
GRAPHICS	LINKS	NEWSLETTER	LAWS/REGS
◆	◆	◆	

Includes:
- What's New
- Research and Information
- Search Engine
- Teaching Center
- Eruption Alerts by LISTSERV

Great site for anyone interested in volcanoes, with lots of current updates and great photo library. Wonderful educational service to explain things to the public.

VOLCANO

International Association of Volcanology and Chemistry of the Earth's Interior (IAVCEI) Home Page			
International Association of Volcanology and Chemistry of the Earth's Interior (IAVCEI)			
http://geont1.lanl.gov/HEIKEN/ONE/IAVCEI_HOME_PAGE.HTM			
GRAPHICS	LINKS	NEWSLETTER	LAWS/REGS
◆	◆		

Includes:
- Publications
- Conferences
- Safety Recommendations
- Links to Related Sites
- Videos

The Association represents the primary international focus for: (1) research in volcanology, (2) efforts to mitigate volcanic disasters, and (3) research into closely related disciplines.

Michigan Technological University (MTU) Volcanoes Home Page			
Michigan Technological University			
http://www.geo.mtu.edu/volcanoes/			
GRAPHICS	LINKS	NEWSLETTER	LAWS/REGS
◆	◆		

Includes:
- Worldwide Volcanic Reference Map
- Recent and Ongoing Activity
- Volcanic Hazards Mitigation
- Remote Sensing of Volcanoes
- Terminology and Definitions
- Links to Related Sites
- Online Journals of Volcanology
- Volcanic Humor

Nice maps, great photos, and useful links. One of the best volcano sites around.

VOLCANO

The Electronic Volcano			
Dartmouth College, New Hampshire			
http://www.dartmouth.edu/~volcano/			
GRAPHICS	LINKS	NEWSLETTER	LAWS/REGS
◆	◆		

Includes:
- Electric Volcano Introduction
- Volcano LISTSERV
- Catalogs of Active Volcanoes
- Datasets for Active Volcanoes
- Electronic Versions of Text Material
- Journals of Volcanology
- Visual Information
- Maps
- Volcanic Observatories/Institutions
- Theses on Volcanism
- Volcanic Hazards
- Current Events and Research
- Volcano Name and Country Index

Has just about everything you would want for finding information about volcanoes: maps, photos, links to other sites.

Montserrat Volcano Updates			
Government of Montserrat and Montserrat Volcano Observatory			
http://www.geo.mtu.edu/volcanoes/west.indies/soufriere			
GRAPHICS	LINKS	NEWSLETTER	LAWS/REGS
◆	◆		

Includes:
- Monteserrat Volcano Observatory
- Other Eruption Updates
- Maps
- Smithsonian Institution Global Volcanism Network Bulletins
- Images
- Links to Related Sites

Stays right on target. Only for this volcano, but has great pictures, maps, links, and is easy to use. Nice design.

VOLCANO

Long Valley Caldera Response Plan page			
U.S. Geological Survey (USGS)			
http://quake.wr.usgs.gov/VOLCANOES/LongValley/Response.html			
GRAPHICS	LINKS	NEWSLETTER	LAWS/REGS
◆	◆		

Includes:

This is text of the U.S. Geological Survey's plan for reducing the risk from volcanic activity in Long Valley in eastern California.

This is critical as an example of a risk reduction program for volcanoes.

Natural Hazards Mitigation Group			
University of Geneva			
http://www.unige.ch/hazards			
GRAPHICS	LINKS	NEWSLETTER	LAWS/REGS
◆	◆		

Includes:
- Natural Hazards Mitigation Studies
- CERG Current News and Information
- Volcanic Hazards Mitigation Team
- Seismic Hazards Mitigation Team
- Volcano Pictures
- Links to Related Sites

Easy to use. Great links. Great pictures. Very unique way of organizing photos. Also provides a link to find grants for mitigation project.

VOLUNTEERS

Emergency Management Information
Volunteers in Technical Assistance
http://www.vita.org/disaster/

GRAPHICS	LINKS	NEWSLETTER	LAWS/REGS
♦	♦		

Includes:

- International Situation Reports
- NVOAD Reports
- Emergency Humanitarian Appeals
- Relief Web
- World Food Program Reports
- International Committee of the Red Cross
- Humanitarian Response Page
- Global Emergency Management Systems
- Disaster Information Center

This is a major link gate for relief-related information and recent reports on disasters.

National Voluntary Organizations Active in Disaster (NVOAD) Home Page
National Voluntary Organizations Active in Disaster (NVOAD)
http://www.vita.org/nvoad

GRAPHICS	LINKS	NEWSLETTER	LAWS/REGS
♦	♦		

Includes:

- Publications
- VOAD Member Information
- Recent Situation Reports
- Membership

Site for connections to ARC, Salvation Army, Catholic Charities, Second Harvest, etc. The best place to go for volunteer interests. Has several great documents, including one on how to organize State VOAD volunteer organizations.

WEATHER

Severe Weather and Natural Disaster Warning Bulletins			
Ohio State University			
http://asp1.sbs.ohio-state.edu/severetext.html			
GRAPHICS	LINKS	NEWSLETTER	LAWS/REGS
	◆		

Includes:
- Severe Weather
- Adverse Marine Weather and Coastal Flooding
- Tropical Advisories and Statements
- Special Weather and Severe Weather Statements
- Adverse Winter Weather
- Flooding, Fog, Wind, Fire, Pollution Advisories
- Avalanche, Earthquake, Ice and Tsunami Reports
- Other Bulletins

Emergency Managers Weather Information Network (EMWIN) Home Page			
National Weather Service (NWS) and Federal Emergency Management Agency (FEMA)			
http://www.nws.noaa.gov/oso/oso1/oso12/document/emwin.htm			
GRAPHICS	LINKS	NEWSLETTER	LAWS/REGS
	◆		

Includes:
- Radio Datastream
- Internet Datastream
- Satellite Datastream
- Commercial Vendors
- Radio Broadcast Areas

This site is formulated for those involved with developing a technical information link to the National Weather Service.

WEATHER

Weather Catalog			
Historic Publications			
http://www.awod.com/weather			
GRAPHICS	LINKS	NEWSLETTER	LAWS/REGS
	◆		

Includes:
- Weather Links
- Posters
- Videos
- Documentaries
- Miscellaneous Weather Items
- Conferences
- Dr. William Gray's Hurricane Predictions

Actually a great link site to other weather information. Tons of things for sale associated with weather: books, posters, videos, slides, clothing, etc.

Yahoo Weather Sites			
Yahoo			
http://www.yahoo.com/Science/Earth_Sciences/Meteorology_Weather/			
GRAPHICS	LINKS	NEWSLETTER	LAWS/REGS
◆	◆		

Includes:
- Today's Weather News
- Yahoo! Weather
- Indexes for All Weather Topics

553 sites you can go to for weather. Outstanding link site.

WEATHER

National Oceanic & Atmospheric Administration (NOAA)			
National Oceanic & Atmospheric Administration (NOAA)			
http://www.noaa.gov/			
GRAPHICS	LINKS	NEWSLETTER	LAWS/REGS
◆	◆		

Includes:
- Mission, Vision and Strategy
- NOAA in the News
- Program Elements
- Access to NOAA Information and Data Services

You have to dig a lot to get to the information. But, if you dig, it's got lots of good data.

National Broadcasting System (NBC) weather information			
National Broadcasting System (NBC)			
http://www.intellicast.com			
GRAPHICS	LINKS	NEWSLETTER	LAWS/REGS
◆	◆		

Includes:
- USA Weather
- World Weather
- Tropical Weather
- Traveler's Advisories
- Ski Reports
- Weather Almanac
- Dr. Dewpoint
- National Parks
- Local Time Check

If you want the latest, and greatest information on weather, here's where I'd start. Let's you link to all the key places you need to go. Fast. Great graphics and info. Great design. A must for all!

WEATHER

National Weather Service (NWS) Weather Warnings			
National Weather Service (NWS)			
http://iwin.nws.noaa.gov/iwin/us/allwarnings.html			
GRAPHICS	LINKS	NEWSLETTER	LAWS/REGS

Includes:
- Actual real-time severe storm warnings

A great site to have up in the EOC during severe weather season in any community.

WeatherNet			
University of Michigan			
http://cirrus.sprl.umich.edu/wxnet/			
GRAPHICS	LINKS	NEWSLETTER	LAWS/REGS
◆	◆		

Includes:
- Feature Links
- Forecasts and Warnings
- Radar and Satellite
- Software Archive
- Travel Cities Weather
- Tropical Weather
- Weather Cameras

This site offers thousands of forecasts for the Weather. What a site! It's got everything. Hardly any need to have any other weather tool on board. This site won every Web Site award around.

WEATHER

Tropical Storm Information Center			
Ohio State University			
http://asp1.sbs.ohio-state.edu/tropicaltext.html			
GRAPHICS	LINKS	NEWSLETTER	LAWS/REGS
◆	◆		

Includes:
- Atlantic Tropical Data
- Pacific Tropical Data
- Indian Tropical Data

Great site. Lots of graphics and information. Easy to use. Well divided into the oceans of the world. This is an important site for predicting long-term weather.

USA Today Thunderstorm Information Index			
USA Today			
http://www.usatoday.com/weather/wtsm0.htm			
GRAPHICS	LINKS	NEWSLETTER	LAWS/REGS
◆	◆		

Includes:
- Types of Thunderstorms
- Lightning and Thunder
- Thunderstorm Precipitation
- Thunderstorm Winds
- Climatology and History
- Other Information
- Links to Related Sites

Has a lot of information, best explanations I've seen on Net of weather phenomena. Very crisp. Lots of great pictures and links. Use this to train yourself, staff, or other interested adults/kids. This site also ties to their other weather education sites.

WEATHER

Project Safeside			
American Red Cross and The Weather Channel			
http://www.weather.com/safeside			
GRAPHICS	LINKS	NEWSLETTER	LAWS/REGS
◆	◆		

Includes:
- Extreme Heat
- Flooding
- Hurricane
- Lightning
- Tornadoes
- Disaster Plan
- Breaking Weather
- U.S. City Forecasts
- International Forecasts
- Maps
- Travel Conditions
- Boat&Beach
- Aviation

This site focuses on weather safety and has valuable materials for educating the public.

Societal Impacts of Weather			
National Center for Atmospheric Research (NCAR)			
http://www.dir.ucar.edu/esig/socasp/			
GRAPHICS	LINKS	NEWSLETTER	LAWS/REGS
◆	◆	◆	

Includes:
- User Groups
- Phenomena
- Economics and Casualty Data
- Community and Research Tools
- Site Information
- What's New
- Links to Related Sites

Home of *WeatherZine*, a bimonthly Internet newsletter.

WEATHER

World Meteorological Organization (WMO)			
United Nations			
http://www.wmo.ch/			
GRAPHICS	LINKS	NEWSLETTER	LAWS/REGS
	♦		

Includes:
- What is WMO
- What's New
- Statements, Press Releases, Announcements
- Strategic Plan
- Major Programs
- Support of Relief Missions
- Data Bases
- Satellite Activity

Lots of active information on a world view of weather and its impacts.

Emergency Action Information			
Collier County Emergency Management (Florida, USA)			
www.collierem.org			
GRAPHICS	LINKS	NEWSLETTER	LAWS/REGS
♦	♦		

Includes:
- Updates on Weather Topics
- Emergency Action Information
- Local County Forecast
- Florida Weather Summary
- Special Weather Statements
- Florida State Forecasts
- Current Radar Image

Good example of what to put on the net for local concerns. County emergency management site.

WEATHER

National Center for Atmospheric Research (NCAR) Digital Media Catalog			
National Center For Atmospheric Research: University Corporation for Atmospheric Research			
http://www.ucar.edu/DMC/DMCHome.html			
GRAPHICS	LINKS	NEWSLETTER	LAWS/REGS
◆	◆		

Includes:
- Climate Change and Pollution
- Clouds
- Computers and Modeling
- Illustrations and Miscellaneous
- NCAR Site and People
- Research Equipment
- Satellite Images
- Solar Images
- Weather and Phenomena

Basically a vending site for incredible color slides which are invaluable for presentations.

System for Technology Exchange for Natural Disasters (STEND)-- (Geneva Switzerland)			
World Meteorological Organization (WMO)			
http://www.wmo.ch/web/homs/stend.html			
GRAPHICS	LINKS	NEWSLETTER	LAWS/REGS
	◆		

Includes:
- Project Description
- Hydrology
- Seismology
- Volcanology

This site is very risk assessment oriented, and also features mitigation information.

WEATHER

NSSL Bibliographic Database			
National Severe Storms Laboratory (NSSL)			
http://doplight.nssl.uoknor.edu/projects/nbd			
GRAPHICS	LINKS	NEWSLETTER	LAWS/REGS

Includes:
- About
- Help

- Add
- Simple Search
- Advanced Search

This site features a library of Winter weather data from 1882-current.

National Severe Storms Laboratory			
National Oceanographic and Atmospheric Administration (NOAA), Norman, Oklahoma			
http://www.nssl.uoknor.edu			
GRAPHICS	LINKS	NEWSLETTER	LAWS/REGS

Includes:
- General Information
- OAR Earth Day Page

- The Weather Room
- Scientific Research
- Real-Time MM5 Forecast

This site is useful for research being done on severe storm planning.

WEATHER

Weather Impacts VJournal			
Weather Impacts VJournal			
http://www.dir.ucar.edu/esig/socasp/vjournal.html			
GRAPHICS	LINKS	NEWSLETTER	LAWS/REGS

Includes:
- 1997
- 1996
- 1995
- 1995 and Prior
- New Additions
- Glossary

This site offers a plethora of research documents on weather and related phenomena.

WXP Weather Processor Home Page			
Purdue University			
http://wxp.atms.purdue.edu/			
GRAPHICS	LINKS	NEWSLETTER	LAWS/REGS
◆	◆		

Includes:
- Information
- Quick Search Engine
- Analyses
- Forecasts
- Miscellaneous Information
- Satellite Imagery

WXP is a software package developed at Purdue University as a general purpose weather visualization tool for current, forecasted and archived meteorological data. This site is for the weather specialist who needs some intense graphical analysis for reports and predictions.

Bright Ideas: Write an e-mail to some of the sites you found most intriguing.

Ask the key contact or webmaster at the site to help you with:

✓ some ideas about how they developed their site,

✓ a listing of the kinds of software or vendors they used; and

✓ what things they did for their site that their readers liked most.

4
Mining the Emergency Web Site Listings

Diamonds Everywhere

If your interests are focused solely on one topic, let me recommend the following references for specific subject areas:

- **Chemistry:**
  Chemical Guide to the Internet, C.C. Lee, 1996, Government Institutes.

- **Waste Management:**
  Recycling and Waste Management Guide to the Internet, Roger Guttentag, 1997, Government Institutes.

- **Environmental:**
  Environmental Guide to the Internet, Carol Briggs-Erickson and Toni Murphy, 1997, Government Institutes.

- **Safety and Health:**
  Safety and Health on the Internet, Ralph B. Stuart, III, 1997, Government Institutes.

Now is a great time to really dig into the huge pile of information you have just been exposed to in Chapter 3—without much guidance. There are strategies to speed your search for information within the master list. These are the little tools for "mining" information, so called by professionals who make their livings finding data on the Internet. For even more ways to find information, please read Chapters 5 and 6.

Strategies for Using the List

Before using the list in Chapter 3 to find your topic, try consulting the extensive index at the end of this book. You might be surprised how fast you can find exactly what you are searching for without having to use any other strategy.

The second strategy is to use the 48 topic titles on the second page of Chapter 3. Enough common emergency management subjects are listed there so that you should be able to find a beginning point for almost any interest. If there isn't a specific title area that seems to make a match, try the section titled "General Topics." This is a sampling of Web Sites that are not a distinct fit into the other sections. These sites often cover a variety of subjects in emergency management.

The third strategy is to look at the first line of each page in the listing. The lists are compiled alphabetically under the 48 topic titles. The topic for the first Web Site on a page precedes the listings. This will help you quickly find your place anywhere in the hundreds of listings.

The fourth strategy is to know what specific type of information you want from a Web Site on the site listings. The tables have been arranged so you can find a number of key factors quickly for every Web Site. These are found in the following order, by line, from the top to the bottom of the listing tables:

1.   Name of the home page

2.   Name of the organization or individual responsible for the material at the Web Site

3.   The URL code so you can enter it into your browser to find the site

Indicators if there are:

> ⇒ Graphics (pictures, maps, tables, etc.)
> ⇒ Links to Related Sites (even if only one)
> ⇒ Newsletter
> ⇒ Laws and Regulations

4.   A listing of some of the topics in the Web Site Table of Contents

5.   A personal comment from the authors about the Web Site quality, content, or usefulness

Evaluating a Web Site at a Glance

There are several other strategies that can save you time once you have found the Web Sites in the listing that you think might be useful. First, look at how much information is listed in the "Includes" area. This is a good bellwether for the complexity and detail in the Web Site. Some Web Sites offer a very narrow focus of information, which may be appropriate. If your focus is narrow as well, that may the best match for your search.

Second, look for Web Sites that have links. By our estimate, if you were to use all the links available from every Web Site in Chapter 3, and then went to every link available from all of those links, you would have access to thousands of home pages. This is far more than any one book could list or track. So, the more links available at a Web Site, the more chances of continuing the trail to eventually finding your treasure trove. It's like a mystery novel. Every new link leads to another clue.

Third, look at the organization responsible for the information. Anyone can place information on the Internet, but you must evaluate for yourself how reliable you rate the originators of the data. If you are using information on the Internet for a report, or for research that can affect public policy, you may be asked to justify your sources.

Fourth, take a moment to read our review of the site. The reviews are subjective but do reflect decades of experience in emergency management. They also may contain notes about offerings in the Web Site that have special merit.

You are now ready to type the URL code into your browser. Double check to make sure it appears exactly like it is printed in the tables. If the Web Site does not open, or your browser says the Web Site is not available, retype the URL and try one more time. If the Web Site is still unavailable, there are three possible reasons:

1. The server for the Web Site is down or unavailable.

2. The Web Site has moved without leaving a forwarding address marker.

3. The Web Site is abandoned.

If the Web Site was defined as critical, and the organization that supported it looks like it had longevity, use the information in Chapter 6 to track down the new location of the Web Site. It doesn't take long, and may prove invaluable.

Once at the Home Page

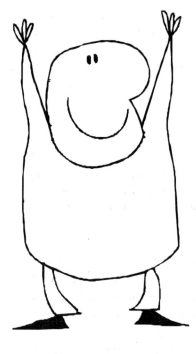

Aaaaah, home sweet home page! You made it! But now you find that the layout of the Web Site doesn't look like the one you saw earlier, or the one before that. Puzzled? You shouldn't be. The World Wide Web is like a city, with all the variety of houses and skyscrapers.

There are a few things you will have to know about Web Site design and structure before proceeding (This will aid you if you want to build your own site someday, as further explained in Chapter 9.) Not all home pages are the same—in fact, very few are similar. This can be a little problematic for those just entering the World Wide Web. When you come to someone's home you expect to see something that looks like a door. Unfortunately, an occasional creative Web Master produces a door that may look like a window, a barred jail cell, or even a black hole. There are several reasons for this diversity, including:

- Software used to design the site;
- Design ideas of the Web Master;
- Variety on the part of the "information holders" who direct the Web Master; and
- Limitations at the ISP server which may have limited home page structure and content.

So, celebrate in the diversity of Web Sites. Consider them all jewels in the mine: beautiful in their own way. But all jewels have some similarities. To help you find just the part of the information you want, we've designed a "blue print" home page that contains many of the kinds of elements you may find. It is rare that all the elements are on a specific home page. By using this as a map, however, you'll be able to look for your treasure that much faster as you encounter the varieties of each Web Site.

The Blue Print

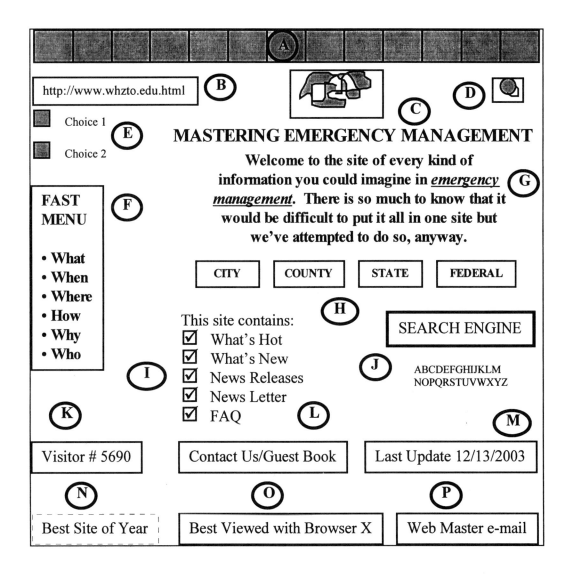

http://www.whzto.edu.html   **B**

Choice 1
Choice 2   **E**

MASTERING EMERGENCY MANAGEMENT

C

D

Welcome to the site of every kind of information you could imagine in *emergency management*. There is so much to know that it would be difficult to put it all in one site but we've attempted to do so, anyway.

G

FAST MENU   **F**

- **What**
- **When**
- **Where**
- **How**
- **Why**
- **Who**

| CITY | COUNTY | STATE | FEDERAL |

H

This site contains:
☑ What's Hot
☑ What's New
☑ News Releases
☑ News Letter
☑ FAQ

I

SEARCH ENGINE

J

ABCDEFGHIJKLM
NOPQRSTUVWXYZ

K

L

M

Visitor # 5690

Contact Us/Guest Book

Last Update 12/13/2003

N

O

P

Best Site of Year

Best Viewed with Browser X

Web Master e-mail

A TYPICAL LAYOUT FOR A HOME PAGE

Description of Each Element

A   The Browser Tool Menu:

This is the guide for your Internet browser software. Here you will find many options that allow you to manipulate and collect information from the World Wide Web, as well as moving back and forth between Web Sites.

B   The URL (Uniform Resource Locator) Code:

This series of numbers, letters and punctuation tells the ISP where to search for a Web Site. This code is as individual for each Web Site as a finger print. Each part of the URL (pronounced "Earl") tells something specific about the Web Site, e.g., the www means it is located on the World Wide Web.

C   The Home Page Title and Graphic:

Most home pages begin with a title frame or heading that clearly identifies the purpose or topic area of the Web Site. This is often accompanied by a logo of the organization or agency.

D   The Sound Selection Key:

Many Web Sites feature voice and music elements. Sound files cause older modems and slower computer systems to slow to a crawl, and in some cases lock up. The user may also have to load an application from the Internet in order to hear the sounds. For these reasons, a well developed site will offer the option of turning the sound files off.

E   Web Site Use Choices:

You may be allowed to choose several options including viewing with/without frames (which puts details in individual, interactive boxes), or to see material without graphics (to speed loading for slower systems). The choices may include asking if your computer supports Java Script, which you may select in the preferences section of the browser software. You may also be asked to load a special software for graphics (e.g., Acrobat™) or sound (e.g. RealAudio™).

F   The Side-Bar Menu in Frames:

Web Sites may automatically structure their data in frames. The key contents of the Web Site are often listed in a side-bar frame on the home page. The choices are usually highlighted or may appear with hot buttons that will lead you to the correct material.

G   Introductory Text and HTML links:

Most home pages open with an introduction to the subject material, and perhaps to the founding organization. There may be highlighted HTML links in the text to lead the reader directly to critical pages, or even to other Web Sites. This is often designed to help a reader who has reached the wrong or inappropriate area, or one who may be looking for a topic related the Web Site.

H   Hot Spot Subject Boxes:

Special boxes with key topics may be set aside early on a home page to assist the reader. This is especially true if the site tends to use few graphics and avoids frames. A hot spot could be encountered anywhere on the Web Site when the cursor goes from looking like this ➞ to this 🖑. When the little hand appears over an area of text, or graphics, it usually means that clicking the mouse will take you to another area of information, or it may enlarge a graphic for better viewing.

I   Table of Contents with HTML Linkage:

One of the most common structures on a home page is a simple bullet listing of the main topics and elements of the Web Site. Each listing is linked to the topic area of interest. These most often include:

- *What's Hot* or *What's New* (usually the latest updated information)
- *About Us* (gives a background description of the organization)
- *FAQ* (Frequently Asked Questions to help you find your information sooner)
- *Graphics*
- *Links*

J   Search Engine with/without Alphabetized Linkages:

Not every home page will offer a search engine for its Web Site. The most common format for those that do, however, is to offer an open subject box that allows open search and/or an alphabetical listing of topic areas.

K   Visitor Census Box:

This option shows a reader a quick total of all the people who have visited the Web Site, usually since a specific reference date. This information is used by the Web Master to prove to the readers that the site is "hot" and worth visiting, and also allows the Web Master an idea of visit trends. This can be an indicator when new materials need to be added to draw more visitors. It can also show when a site is being overwhelmed.

L   Contact Bar and Guest Registration Book:

Many originating organizations like to know about the kinds of visitors who view their sites. This enables them to tailor the Web Site to the needs of the public. There is often an e-mail contact listed that allows you to send e-mail directly to the organization. The authors have found this capability invaluable when searching for a obscure subject. It ties you directly to many people behind the scenes you might not know, or not know how to reach.

M   Last Update Log

Well organized, thoughtful Web Masters will place a clear marker at the home page to let readers know the last time the Web Site was updated. This saves you time, if you are aware of the last time you visited. It is also a telling sign of a Web Site that is abandoned. When there has not been a update for months (or years) it is a clear indicator that any information on the site will be of minimal value.

N   Web Site Awards

Formerly, awards posted at a site were of value to the Internet surfer. However, so many sites have posted counterfeit or imaginary awards that there is little value in looking for them.

O   Browser Guidance

Some Web Sites will suggest the type of Internet browser software that works best with their site. The authors have found limited value to this recommendation. Most commercial browsers are so similar now that there is little trouble viewing most Web Sites with a variety of softwares.

P   E-mail connection to the Web Site Web Master

There is always value in communicating with the Web Site Web Master. You might be able to find a good contact to the organization through an unposted e-mail. You might also find out how you can post information about your organization, or get permission to use the materials or graphics on the Web Site. Remember, many Web Sites are copyrighted, and your use or misuse of their materials falls under the copyright protection laws.

So What Else Can You Do at the Web Site?

As stated earlier, this book is not designed to explain how specific computer elements or software work. There are many other texts that do that. However, you should be aware of just some of the wonderful tools that your Internet browser makes available to you, such as:

- Saving the URL codes and home page titles as bookmarks that you can store in your own library, and organize in folders according to your needs.

- E-mailing the home page or Web Site to another computer.

- Copying the materials from a Web Site into your word processor, and saving it as a file you can later use for reference and reports.

- Capturing photos and graphics for your reports or for your own Web site.

- Printing the Web Site completely.

- Chatting with other emergency management professionals through the Web Site chat area.

- Sending e-mail directly from the Internet browser.

And that is just the beginning. For some practical applications, try using the exercises in Chapter 8 to hone your Internet research skills for emergency management.

Bright Ideas: Meet with your staff on an Internet chat site at least once every 6 months and hold a "virtual" staff meeting.

Ask your staff to:

✓ practice using their skills at sending and receiving e-mail while chatting;

✓ send graphics and home page URLs; and

✓ send a voice greeting over e-mail.

5
Making it Work for You

The Need for Horsepower

If there is a single maxim that emergency management personnel must live by today it is "DO IT NOW!" Paperwork, payments, production and planning are more complicated each day. The seasonal rest periods that were once a hiatus for catch-up work are gone. Even the holidays are pressured by the constant push to get more and more preparations in place for larger and more complex disaster operations. In the middle of this flurry is the need for faster and more accurate access to information. If the Web Site lists in Chapter 3 were the mine, and the strategies in Chapter 4 were methods to guess where the ore might be located, then this chapter is surely of the tunnels in the mine—which turns to take if you want planning and preparedness, response, relief, recovery or mitigation nuggets from the veins of the Internet. It will substantially speed your efforts if you know which parts of the list to turn to for each major function of emergency management. This knowledge can be reinforced by using the exercises in Chapter 8 to evaluate your proficiency at finding information about specific functions of emergency management.

Planning and Preparedness

Planning precedes preparedness: it is important to first develop a comprehensive "Plan" that incorporates overall strategies and management policies. The Plan should contain general concepts and strategies at the highest level of cooperation within and between agencies. It is then supported by a variety of procedures providing specific data and tactical information about emergency and disaster response, relief, recovery and mitigation.

Preparedness involves all actions necessary to ready materials, facilities and personnel involved with response, relief, recovery and mitigation. This is an extensive effort which can include construction and/or renovation of emergency operations centers, decontamination centers, communications facilities and response vehicles. Equipment preparedness runs the gamut from pens and pencils to hazmat suits and mainframe computers. Personnel are prepared through formal training classes and hands-on experiences in drills and exercises. None of these actions can occur unless the goals and strategies of the organization are defined in the Plan. Preparedness provides the supporting procedures to ensure that operating tactics are in place to execute the emergency management strategies.

The list in Chapter 3 opens several doorways to preparedness resources. One of the major benefits of investigating a variety of organizations on the World Wide Web is to gain access to their existing Plan and procedures. Most government agencies are more than willing to provide electronic copies of their documents, since the effort was paid for by tax dollars. Sections of documents may be deleted or withheld (e.g., if they contain sensitive information, such as security issues or Continuity of Government specifications). However, anything that is publicly available at a local library (as supplied by a government agency) should be made available if requested correctly through an organization's home page. This technique is both a tremendous time-saving and quality improvement tool, since each agency takes approaches to the same issues. It allows true cross-pollination of concepts across state and international boundaries.

Many key sources are listed under preparedness in Chapter 3, including the following:

- **State and Local Guide for All Hazard Emergency Operations Planning** is one of the key standards for planning and preparednes in the US. The information checklists here are the basics for constructing all of the key elements of a community or agency plan.

- **Canadian Centre for Emergency Preparedness** provides a training link needed to complete preparedness activities.

- **"How To" Fact Sheets for Disaster Preparedness** are FEMA documents critical to preparing the public about the key elements found in the Plan and procedures.

- **Report: Natural Disaster Reduction: A Plan for the Nation** is a critical document with an agenda and philosophy which should be incorporated in all plans and procedures for emergency management.

- **Emergency Preparedness Information Exchange (EPIX)** is a key site for finding research information to substantiate and enhance your plans and preparedness activities.

- **Natural Hazards** is a site that focuses on a variety of hazards so that you can develop some approaches to special procedures or annexes for such risks as tornado, earthquake, fire, flood, hurricane, etc.

Response

Previously, most emergency managers would not consider using the Internet during response. However, this trend is quickly changing. More and more emergency operations centers have open lines to weather services, flood information, news bureaus and a host of other information providers that give instant updates of information critical to the successful deployment and direction of field operations.

In the future, the Internet will provide even better and more services for response operations, as discussed in Chapter 10. The Internet is also going to offer the greatest potential for the true integration of local, state and federal interests during large regional events. With instantaneous sharing of information, such as using the Response Information Management System (**RIMS**) in California, there is a growing tendency to use the Internet as a backbone for redundant, if not primary, communications.

The sites provided in the Chapter 3 list focus on several elements associated with response, including:

- **Communication**
- **Law Enforcement**
- **Fire**

- **Health/Medical**
- **Hazardous Materials**
- **Search and Rescue**

There are far too many sites for each element to list them here. It is worth the time and effort to investigate the elements, depending on the response discipline you are coordinating during Plan and procedure preparation, and for drill/exercise planning. There is no lack of information on the Internet for these emergency management subjects, since many related links are provided for them on Web Sites.

Relief

Emergency managers have struggled with defining the lines between response and recovery. More plans (including those from FEMA) are beginning to include Relief as a transition phase between response and recovery. Relief functions as this bridge in the emergency management cycle.

Relief entails the gathering of resources to accommodate the needs of people and animals. The entire process of evacuation, mass care and shelter, feeding, medical care, long-term housing, and return to the community are included. Relief focuses intensely on the suffering of both humans and non-humans gathered by chance after a calamity.

Chapter 3 lists sites that address relief issues, including the following:

- **Mass Relocation Project** is a developing site dealing with plans to prepare model regional mass care and shelter facilities for the public after large-scale catastrophic events. The plans include considerations for medically needy evacuees, pets and livestock, and special designs to meet the Americans with Disabilities Act (**ADA** requirements.

- **International Committee of the Red Cross (ICRC)** is a major site for assessing progress in major relief campaigns, and approaches to handling current or planned campaigns in any region of the world.

- **International Emergency and Refugee Health Program** is a site with strong focus on the continued health care and disease prevention in mass care and shelter situations, expecially when there may be long-term encampments of evacuees.

- **Relief Now** is a central source of information on faith-based relief work, which has started to rival government response in scope of complexity, size and total support.

- **Relief Web** is a key link to all major relief activities carried on and supported by the United Nations and affiliated organizations.

- **National Emergency Resource Information Network (NERIN)** is a developing site that promises to tie together the resource base of community-based organizations (**CBOs**) throughout the U.S., so that local government participants can quickly assess the total arsenal of quality tools available to serve the public's need during relief.

Recovery

Much of the groundwork of successful recovery is done in the planning and preparedness stage. Recovery operations must appear seamless to the operation of community life in order for normalcy to return. This is critical for the continuity of culture, government, and general societal stability. Recovery involves the support of citizen needs through restoration of infrastructure, e.g., debris removal and repair of roads, water drainage and building reconstruction, and utility and government service restoration.

The list in Chapter 3 lends some unique ideas for preparing for recovery, especially in the business sector, including the following examples:

- **Disaster Recovery Journal** is a site that offers superior resources to address any imaginable challenge in business contingency work.

- **Contingency Planning and Disaster Recovery** is offered by RiskInfo with another mountain of references and information on business recovery.

- **Business Recovery Manager's Association (BRMA)** offers not only critical information and examples of how to prepare for recovery, but also a direct connection to the kinds of people who know this field.

- **Basic Business Recovery Plan** is offered by the Massachusetts Institute of Technnology. This could be used as a boiler plate for almost any organization when planning for recovery actions to restore their operations.

- **Updates on Planning for Disaster Recovery** is offered by the International City/County Management Association (**ICMA**). This site represents one of the oldest government associations in the world, and certainly is a source for a world of real-life experience in successful recovery operations at the local government level.

- **Toolkit for Crisis Prevention, Mitigation and Recovery in Africa (CPMR)** offers a much larger perspective on recovery when entire countries have to be rebuilt and reconstructed after catastrophic natural or man-made events.

Mitigation

Mitigation has been the stepchild of the emergency management process. Often touted as the answer, but seldom implemented when needed, the time has come for mitigation to take on a powerful new life of its own. Perhaps the greatest factor driving the new considerations for "preventing a disaster before it happens" is the huge loss to insurance companies during the last ten years of U.S. catastrophes. Floods, earthquakes and hurricanes have forced insurers (including the federal government) to clamp down hard on repetitive community development planning mistakes, both in rural and urban settings.

The concept of mitigation is certainly not new in the U.S. The vision of the U.S. Corps of Engineers, through their dam programs, has saved untold human lives and property. The Internet was also a mitigation project, one to ensure the continued operation of a communications network in case of nuclear attack. Without mitigation planning, the World Wide Web might not exist today. These mitigation commitments, and others, have helped make the United States financially stable and productive.

Though mitigation was once difficult to investigate on the Internet, it is now well represented by a growing number of Web Site references, many of which are at the Federal Emergency Management Agency home page. Some examples are listed below:

- **Federal Emergency Management Agency (FEMA) Mitigation Directorate** offers the best mitigation guidance for the emergency management community in the United States. However, much of this material could be used in any country.

- **International Center for Disaster Mitigation Engineering (INCEDE)** is offered by the University of Tokyo, Japan. The Japanese have strong impetus to ensure the structural integrity of their cities. This site offers a gateway into that mitigation planning as the Japanese strive to prevent the huge losses caused by the Tokyo and Kobe quakes.

- **Conference Site: Practical Solutions to Protect Cities at Risk** is a now-completed on-line conference about the mitigation efforts needed to protect city dwellers world wide. The United Nations supports these efforts.

Reports (After Action Reports and Research)

After the recovery phase is started, you will undoubtedly have to begin the process of writing tedious reports and blindingly dull investigation papers. This is a time for deciding how to explain what happened by digging through many records, public and private, as well as investigating how other organizations prepared reports in the past that lead to successful outcomes with the public and regulators. It is one of the most painful realities of the emergency management business (especially since most of the documents soon take up space and dust on a shelf until a politician needs them for fodder after the next disaster). But since there is no escaping the process, you should be able to use the tools of the World Wide Web to advantage to enhance the contents, and shorten the process. There are a number of tools provided in the list of Web Sites.

There are two type of tools in the list. First, there are the pure writing and reference tools that are used to increase the quality of the writing. These include, under the topic "Tools":

- **Hypertext Webster Dictionary**
- **Bartlett's Quotations**
- **Roget's Thesaurus**
- **Cybermaps**
- **MapQuest**
- **National Yellow Pages**
- **Zip Code Finder**
- **City Net**

The second type of tool is under the topics "Emergency Management" and under "Research." These sites have libraries of information and powerful search engines that can often find just the fact, figure or concept your need. Some of the Web Sites included in these group are:

- **Natural Hazards Research and Applications Center (Boulder, Colorado)**
- **Natural Hazards Research Centre (NHRC)**
- **What's New at the Federal Emergency Management Agency (FEMA)**
- **GALENET**
- **Government Institutes**
- **General Accounting Office (GAO) Reports Online**
- **Global Emergency Management Service (GEMS)**

Building Reference Libraries—Maps, Documents, Data, Graphics

You'll find yourself chipping away slowly, and tediously at each new project if you haven't developed a reference library of bookmarks for each of the sites you've used.   This is where the real time-saving is apparent. You will amaze others when you can retrieve information in a flash because you've been through the caverns of the mine before.

One solid approach to start with is to build a set of folders in your bookmark file that reflects the topic titles in Chapter 3. You will undoubtedly enhance this listing by putting sub-categories in folders within the main topic folders. You might become crazed if you carry this too far, but the authors have noted at least one of their subject folders that has dozens of sub-categories—and that's weather. Weather has so many references on the World Wide Web, and so many sub-topic areas, that it requires more effort to arrange them all efficiently. For instance, just this year (1997), we built a complete new folder under weather dealing with the El Niño effect.

In addition to the sites that are so valuable, there are also the treasures that you can collect and have at your beck and call for other uses such as reports, presentations, or your own Web Site. What topics should be built onto your computer files? We suggest the following:

- Photographs taken of various disasters, especially weather phenomena

- Charts, graphs, and drawings that explain topics in emergency management

- Cartoons that relate to emergencies and disasters

- Clip art found on the Web Sites

- Maps of key events

- Complete documents, loaded into your favorite word processor, so you have instant access to them in the future (remember, sites do disappear and they do remove material you may have wanted)

- Databases of critical information offered by the Web Sites

Bright Ideas: Start building a chart of the use of Web Sites most useful to your organization during each stage of emergency management.

Divide your staff into teams for each step and ask them to:

✓ compile lists of useful Web Sites,

✓ place the Web Sites in tables that explain their value and their use; and

✓ draw a flow chart of how the Sites relate to specific concerns.

6
How to Find More and More

The Best Kept Secrets

Emergency managers want the best methods to get
the gold fast and accurately. But, the best kept secrets of the
Internet miners are usually out of the way, and often hidden
behind complicated terminology and concepts. This chapter
will be different. In just a few minutes of reading you will be
able to speed through the jargon of power searching on the
Internet. You'll be the envy of the office and the brain trust
for your superiors. The strategies are easy to use and are
provided from the simplest to the slightly more complex. Try
one idea a day and in two weeks you will be an Internet power
surfer.

E-Mail: Simple But Powerful

Very few texts really express the total power of e-mail. It can be a profound
source of quick and accurate information. It can, like a mine collapse, also bury you in a
mound of useless dust and dirt. Learning to manage e-mail for emergency management
is one of the key skills for any emergency manager in today's electronic forum.

The first strategy is to get e-mail. How? First, as you explore the many Web
sites in Chapter 3, look for an e-mail address for the organization that supports the site.
If one is not apparent, e-mail the Web Master and ask for the organization's e-mail
address. Second, every time you meet people involved with your work, ask for their e-

mail address. If they don't have one, ask them for one when they do acquire an address. Finally, ask associates for lists of people they consider valuable contacts who have e-mail access. These three techniques should help you build a file of several hundred addresses within a short time.

But just acquiring e-mail addresses does not mean you have a viable resource. To really enhance the power of e-mail to assist you, try some of the following ideas:

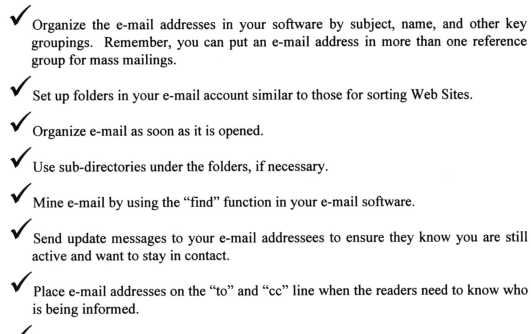

✔ Organize the e-mail addresses in your software by subject, name, and other key groupings. Remember, you can put an e-mail address in more than one reference group for mass mailings.

✔ Set up folders in your e-mail account similar to those for sorting Web Sites.

✔ Organize e-mail as soon as it is opened.

✔ Use sub-directories under the folders, if necessary.

✔ Mine e-mail by using the "find" function in your e-mail software.

✔ Send update messages to your e-mail addressees to ensure they know you are still active and want to stay in contact.

✔ Place e-mail addresses on the "to" and "cc" line when the readers need to know who is being informed.

✔ Place e-mail addresses on the "bcc" line when you use mass mailings. A huge section of e-mail addresses irritates many readers and also makes your list vulnerable to abuse.

✔ Learn to use the "filter" function in your e-mail software.

The filter function is one of the best time savers when using e-mail, especially once you've become a member of a LISTSERV or Newsgroup. The filter allows you to block access to your e-mail account. This can be crucial to avoid the dreaded "spam mail." Advertisements may begin to fill up your daily logs of e-mail if you don't filter out unwanted messages. If you have trouble with this function, contact your department's Information Technology Specialist. He or she will be able to set it up for you.

Finally, learn to archive e-mail. Don't keep building folders year after year with information that is no longer valuable. Make an effort to clear out garbage mail at least every six months, with a much more aggressive cleaning at the beginning of each January to start the year out right.

If your e-mail addresses are up to date, you have a tremendous research and assistance tool you can call on at any time—even in the middle of response. A short note to a dozen key individuals, asking for solutions to a problem you have never encountered before, can yield results quickly and effectively. It might not work every time, but like any tool, it provides you with more options.

Now, we will explore some other magnificent tools that will make your e-mail come alive for emergency management.

LISTSERV (e-mail groups on BITNET)

What is a LISTSERV?

You can cooperate collectively with others using e-mail to share volumes of brief, personalized information on almost any subject. This is best accomplished through a LISTSERV. A LISTSERV is a computer location dedicated to collecting e-mail messages from many people subscribing to a computer operator who then automatically transmits all the messages to all the subscribers at once. This is mainly done on a system of computer connections that preceded the Internet, known as the BITNET. There are over five thousand LISTSERV information sites on the BITNET.

How Do You Get Access?

You need to subscribe to a server to obtain access. This is usually free and simply requires sending an e-mail system to the LISTSERV operator with words such as, "Subscribe."

There are two very different communication patterns when you deal with a LISTSERV. First, there are messages to the system operator. The only messages that should be sent there are requests to subscribe or to stop your subscription. You may also inquire for instructions on how to best communicate in the e-mail forum.

The LISTSERV information area is where you will post questions or comments. You can also browse through other subscribers' comments.

LISTSERV Protocols

The protocols for using e-mail on the Internet are referred to as "netiquette." For instance, it is bad netiquette to send your subscription message or your "unsubscribe" message to the information area. That would mean your administrative request would go to everyone on the LISTSERV. Some sites are populated by users who take this faux pas personally. They may send you angry "flame mail" and overwhelm your e-mail with "mail bombs" (which can be huge, time and space consuming files). So, please make sure you use the correct e-mail address for the right part of the LISTSERV.

If your are a little concerned about how the LISTSERV protocols work, you may want to just watch and monitor the traffic for a while before jumping into the waters. This is called "lurking." There is no rule that says that you must participate. It is estimated that over half the subscribers usually lurk, for whatever reason. Then when you are comfortable, you to can start sending out those interesting questions and answers for all to see. One of the other niceties of the LISTSERV environment is that it is more formal and less free-wheeling than the Newsgroup forums (see below). So, you are likely to find a more professional, well thought-out answer in this arena. However, you may also receive answers that are politically cleansed as well, which is not always the best type of information for all topic areas in emergency management.

Managing the Traffic

Another concern is volume of messages. We've had to unsubscribe more than once when a particularly popular LISTSERV started generating over a hundred e-mail messages a day. One way to work through this much volume is to read instructions from the LISTSERV to find out how to request a digest each day, instead of all the messages. With a digest you can quickly browse for key information. If there is none, just trash the digest. If there is a message you want, note its exact reference number or name and then request it separately. NOTE: LISTSERV sites do not become a running archive of messages. If you don't check for the messages posted, they are soon replaced with new information traffic. Information on the LISTSERV is timely and ephemeral. Newsgroups, on the other hand, leave the messages up for long periods, which makes them particularly valuable for information mining long after a subject was discussed in a particular topic area.

Finding the Servers

How do you find these LISTSERV sites? There are several options. First, there are a few listed in the Chapter 3 Web Sites. The Web Sites act as a doorway to the LISTSERV. These examples include:

- **Research-it**

- **The Electronic Volcano**

There is also a particularly useful site for finding emergency management LISTSERV sites. Use the Web Site: **Emergency Services Database** at: http://www.district.north-van.bc.ca/admin/depart/fire/ffsearch/mainmenu.cfm

LISTERSERV sites can also be invaluable for keeping up-to-date with the latest information releases. One example is the U.S. Government Accounting Office (GAO), which produces many titles each year that are invaluable to government operations, including emergency management. To use the GAO LISTSERV you would begin by sending an e-mail to **majordomo@www.gao.gov.** Just like all of the LISTSERV sites, this will begin your subscription process.

LISTSERV sites also connect emergency managers directly with regulators and policy makers. Sometimes policy evolves through the discussions, and you can watch that occur, or participate. A specific example is The Western States Seismic Policy Council (**WSSPC**). They maintain an e-mail discussion list (WSSPC-l) to support deliberations about seismic policy. To join the WSSPC-l LISTSERV, send an e-mail message to majordomo@nisee.ce.berkeley.edu with the message "subscribe wsspc-l" followed directly by your e-mail address.

You can also find the latest LISTSERV sites through search engines (see below) by typing in words like "LISTSERV" or "e-mail lists." Or, you can use a search engine devoted specifically to LISTSERV sites, such as:

Liszt, the mailing list directory found at:
http://www.liszt.com/

The Internet Tour Bus found at:
http://csbh.mhv.net/~bobrankin/tourbus/

One of the best explanations of use of an emergency management LISTSERV is found in *Safety and Health on the Internet*, Ralph B. Stuart, III, 1997, Government Institutes. Mr. Stuart explains his involvement on the formation of the SAFETY LISTSERV. If you are serious about using other forums in the Internet for emergency management information, then you must have this text. It is invaluable.

Newsgroups (e-mail groups on UseNet)

What is a Newsgroup?

In the beginnings of cyberspace, when users wanted to exchange ideas in a static forum they used the UseNet as the structure of choice. It is simply another way of grouping ideas and thoughts of people utilizing the Internet. Since it is the oldest such forum on the Internet, it is also the largest. No one is sure exactly how many Newsgroups are now available, but it is not unusual for a large server to have as many as 10,000 Newsgroups sited. The Newsgroups contain only ASCII text. Other information, such as graphics, is stored in separate files that have to be selected and transferred to your computer before they can be opened.

How Do You Get Access?

There is no formal subscription to a Newsgroup, like there is for a LISTSERV. However, not all Newsgroups are openly available. You may need to acquire access from the "host" server's operator. The only other restriction to your use of these resources is a newsreader software or online service that will permit you to open the files. The Web browser software you use may also have this option. If not, contact an Information Technology Specialist to find out what your organization is using for Newsgroup entry. You may also get Newsgroup information through search engine queries. Note that some search engines specifically ask if a search is for the World Wide Web or for Newsgroups. This is a powerful tool which can find references completely unavailable on the World Wide Web.

Newsgroup Protocols

The volume of information found on the UseNet requires strict organization techniques so that the data does not become a jumbled, unrecognizable mass. Like a LISTSERV, a server becomes the repository for these e-mail messages, but the hierarchy and classification of concepts is different. The subject areas are placed in domains, using terms similar to URL codes. The upper level domains include such titles as "alt" for alternative, "biz" for business, and "rec" for recreational. It takes a little study once you are in Newsgroup listings to find your area of interest. The upper domain listings are:

alt.	Alternative groups
biz.	Business
clari.	Clarinet commercial services
comp.	Computer discussions
misc.	Any topic that doesn't fit the other domain titles
news.	Discussions about the UseNet
rec.	Recreational activities (e.g., sports and hobbies)
sci.	Scientific discussions
soc.	Social issues

Managing the Traffic

The advantage of Newsgroups is that you do not have to sort through e-mail that arrives each day. Instead, you search through someone else's server that is the repository of the e-mail messages already organized into the domain folders. What you will have to learn, to be most effective in Newsgroups, is how to "upload" files and "download" files that are more than just an e-mail message. These files may be parts of databases, large documents or operational files such as graphics programs, games, etc. The caveat here is to beware of the dreaded virus. Many of the worst cases of viral infections have come from careless downloading of files from Newsgroups. Computer viruses are less likely (but not unknown) to happen when using the World Wide Web.

Finding the Servers

How do you find a listing of the Newsgroups? The best way is through a UseNet-aware search engine. **AltaVista™** and **Excite™** work well for this purpose (see below). Many computer magazines also feature specialty areas for Newsgroups. It is also useful to contact your Internet Service Provider to find out what Newsgroups they support on their server. Another great source of information is the *Internic News*, an online magazine about the Internet and Newsgroups. It is found at: http://rs.internic.net/nic-support/nicnews/

You can also use the following Web sites to help you find Newsgroups:

NetPages™ for finding business (Blue NetPages), individuals (White NetPages), or classified advertising in Acrobat™ (Yellow NetPages) found at: http://www.aldea.com/wwwindex.html

Internic White Pages Directory Services found at:
http://www.internic.net/ds/dspgwp.html

Liszt, the mailing list directory found at:
http://www.liszt.com/

Tile.Net
http://www.tile.net

The Internet Tour Bus found at:
http://csbh.mhv.net/~bobrankin/tourbus/

Bulletin Board Services

Another source of information outside the Web, but still on the Internet, are the Bulletin Board Services (**BBS**). This book focuses on the World Wide Web, and most of the information you will need can be found there. However, due to the continued use of Bulletin Boards, we believe it is necessary to mention them. Access is provided by a call-up number in which you use software to dial directly to a server. The BBS providers use other parts of the Internet, such as FIDONET (mail networking only) and TELNET to interconnect between other BBS sites. These systems are mostly local in scope and provide message downloading, file access and live chat. Their value to emergency management is found in providing specialized information sites for organizations that do not have Internet access through an ISP, or who are not Internet literate. Bulletin boards are usually very simple, with little graphical presentation. This helps support organizations that use older hardware, such as 9600 BAUD modems. Some important World Wide Web sites began as BBS sites, such as SALEMDUG, HMIX and a number of sites for fire and law enforcement.

Newsletters

Knowing the latest information is one thing. Knowing the most important information is another story. Thankfully, there are a number of organizations that cover emergency management with superb online newsletters that summarize and highlight critical information. The tables in Chapter 3 specify if a site has a newsletter. Please look for these under your specific subject of interest.

We recommend the following World Wide Web newsletters for comprehensive information gathering:

- *Stonefly* at NASA

- SALEMDUG

- Natural Hazards Research Center

- Journal of Disaster Research

- FEMA

Chat Areas

There are plenty of live discussion areas on the Web. These are usually referred to as chat sites. While there are not many specifically designed for emergency management, we recommend the following sites as places to occasionally meet other emergency management specialists:

- EIIP found at:
http://www.emforum.org

- SALEMDUG found at:
http://www.salemdug.dis.anl.gov

- Hazardous Materials Information Exchange (**HMIX**) found at:
http://www.hmix.dis.anl.gov/

What Is IRC?

Beyond the Web is an entire world of chat known as Internet Relay Chat (**IRC**). The IRC is a huge network of worldwide users who use other parts of the Internet for immediate written communications. This part of the Internet utilizes large separate networks such as Undernet, DALnet and EFnet, to name just a few of the larger ones.

How Do You Get Access?

Software is the first step to access. There are two primary programs for using the IRC in a PC platform: mIRC and Pirch. Of these two, mIRC is the most commonly used. Next you'll need to know which IRC network server you want to use. There are no other restrictions. (Ircle and Homer are the two common clients for Macintosh systems. UNIX systems usually have built-in IRC software.)

CHAT Protocols

Chat is live, and with that in mind, it's valuable to know that netiquette is critical. These are not cold, static e-mail messages. You are having a conversation by typing and it should be handled the same way as a telephone call. In fact, there are chat areas available now that use the Internet's capacity to carry both voice and video transmission (see Chapter 10). So, it is important that you use your best judgment when chatting with others.

Some chat areas allow members to use pseudonyms, not unlike the handles popular during the CB-radio craze. Most emergency management sites, however, require your real name, which reduces rude behavior. If you do encounter unacceptable behavior, you have the option of asking the system operator to restrict access of the party. They can then be filtered from the chat area.

IRC networks are vast and they have developed their own protocols and commands. It is critical to learn this system before stepping into IRC for they have their own culture, just as Newsgroups and LISTSERV sites maintain unique cultures.

Finding the Chat Rooms

We highly recommend that you visit some of the Web Sites that can prepare you for your IRC experience. They will also help you learn how to find the right "chat room" and communications "channels" for emergency management. Some excellent choices would be:

All About IRC found at:
http://www.psyber.com:80/technology/irc.html

Links and References About IRC found at:
http://web2.airmail.net:80/risingsu/irclinks.html

Conferences/Forums

A growing area of emergency management information exchange is occurring through on-line forums and conferences. What is the difference? A forum is usually open for an extended time and allows continued input by e-mail or by messages within a site server. A conference is usually set up for a day or two and allows live input by direct typing in a chat format.

The best way to become part of these activities is to watch for announcements in the on-line Internet newsletters. There are often special forums that are announced by FEMA, the UN, and by special interest organizations for fire, law, search and rescue, non-profit organizations, and research groups.

An example of a conference advertisement is provided below:

For more information about WSSPC, the WSSPC-1 mailing list, and the upcoming WSSPC annual conference, contact WSSPC, 121 Second Street, Fourth Floor, San Francisco, CA 94105; (415) 974-6435; fax: (415) 974-1747; e-mail: wsspc@wsspc.org; WWW: http://www.wsspc.org.

An example of a forum announcement, with guidelines, is provided below:

DisastMH e-mail discussion forum serves as on ongoing conference for disaster mental health professionals. Through DisastMH, colleagues can discuss mental health issues in disaster preparedness, disaster response, and disaster recovery. (However, individuals needing professional assistance are asked to seek mental health professionals in their own geographic area.)

Relevant topics may include but are not limited to:

- Planning, development, and operations of disaster mental health
- Volunteer issues of solicitation, maintaining interest, recognition
- DMH and interfacing with agencies, schools, government, etc.
- Construction of protocols for disaster response
- Handbook preparation and maintaining records
- Training issues including American Red Cross training, critical incident stress debriefing, and other models
- Issues of risk management (referral systems, liability, safety, etc.)
- Ethical considerations
- Media and public relations issues

- Debriefings and interventions for disaster response
- Communication trees and classification of volunteers
- DMH leadership issues at local, state, national levels
- Clinical issues for disaster response
- Clearinghouse for material available in disaster psychology
- Peer consulting for disaster mental health services
- Communication regarding DMH during an ongoing disaster

If you are a mental health professional or invited associate in disaster psychology, you are welcome to this forum. To subscribe, send the following message to listserv@maelstrom.stjohns.edu:

subscribe DisastMH [first name] [last name]

For example: subscribe DisastMH B.F. Skinner

For additional information, contact the list owner/moderator: Denruth Lougeay, Ph.D.; e-mail: deneelou@znet.com.

ϰ

Forums and conferences are powerful ways to discover the latest breaking news and policy from the people who are at the cutting edge of emergency management. When well organized, these events ensure you have access to the experts and their best information. On-line forums and conferences are replacing many of the traditional national conferences due to the costs of travel and restricted budgets.

Agency Updates

Some organizations allow you to subscribe to a news service that sends updates to your computer via e-mail. It is similar to a LISTSERV, but in this case you don't send messages to the server, and you don't necessarily get messages every day. The messages are usually only those that concern late breaking news. We have learned to approach agency updates by asking:

- What is their value to our area of emergency management?

- How timely are the announcements?

- Are there critical warnings that would impact my operations?

Almost all of the largest emergency management organizations offer such services (e.g., the UN and FEMA). But other, smaller, niche organizations are just as likely to provide e-mail updates. One example of such an offer is provided below:

Ongoing Situation Reports are reports or "sitreps" from the Volunteers in Technical Assistance' (VITA) e-mail LISTSERV. The sitreps include information concerning global disasters as well as relief efforts. If you wish to subscribe to the e-mail LISTSERV and receive the sitreps yourself, send an e-mail message to incident@vita.org.

Search Engines

What is more powerful than a speeding locomotive? A search engine, of course. If you take no other advice from this chapter than to use search engines, you will still be light years ahead of many of those around you. Search engines pull the ore out of the mine and reduce your time hauling heavy loads. They can show you exactly where the great information is located, and quickly. But you have to know what these work horses can do, know where to find them and how to communicate with them.

What Is a Search Engine?

A search engine is a dynamic index, like the Dewey Decimal System, or the Library of Congress numbering system. These indexes look for key words that describe the information you want and then list the Internet sites where you can find the specific referenced data. For instance, you might look for all the information on disasters by simply entering the word "disaster" into a search engine, and then let the software do the work for you. Soon you'll have a huge list of places to visit to complete your research, not unlike using a library card catalog to find a book in the library.

Ten years ago it took the skills of a linguist to find specific information on the Internet. Then the University of Minnesota developed a smart search tool called "Gopher" (after the University mascot). This was followed by improvements, like "Veronica." These tools are still available, but are not as user friendly as the new indexes. They are also much slower. Their real advantage is their thoroughness and capacity for searching many areas not included on other search engines.

There has been great excitement in the last five years as new graphical interfaces have become available for search engines. Tools like Yahoo™, Excite™, and AltaVista™ have become the leaders in search technology. New computer hardware has enabled much faster access to servers for much more time-effective inquiries. This has made the World Wide Web a powerful resource for sharing information and opened its use to almost anyone.

How Do I Learn To Use a Search Engine?

The best way to learn how to use search engines is to play with each one. Most have help files that will assist you with the structure used at that site for search protocols. You'll learn that you can improve searches by making your inquiries very specific. For example, if you entered the word "disaster," as mentioned before, you might get a list of 1500 references. That can be daunting when you have a time limit. You'll learn how to focus the searches by adding restricting terms, e.g., "disasters" plus "U.S." plus "1960" plus "reports" minus "floods." Now you'll get references that should give you U.S. disaster reports, other than floods, for 1960. Try finding that information in five minutes at your local library!

How Do I Find Search Engines?

To save time, you can go to single sites that serve as gateways to many of the most popular search engines. This reduces the time you would use surfing back and forth between the search engine sites. We recommend the use of **All-in-One Search Page** found at:

http://www.albany.net/allinone/

Another great starting point is **Search the Net!** This site is a source of search engines for World Wide Web, UseNet, and many other areas of interest. It is at:

wysiwyg://8/http://www2.gol.com/users/steve/f_search.htm

One more option is the interesting array of search tools offered by the vendor Alden Electronics found at:

http://alden.com/surf.html

Here are examples of some of the search engines on the Internet. Each has its own flavor for searches. Be sure to click on the help section for search techniques and strategies. These strategies vary by each site. The sites highlighted below are ones we find most useful on a daily basis for general searches.

http://altavista.digital.com
http://ftp.cs.princeton.edu/~dwallach/tifaq
http://guide.infoseek.com
http://index.opentext.net
http://webcrawler.com
http://www.achoo.com
http://www.excite.com
http://www.healthatoz.com
http://www.hotbot.com
http://www.looksmart.com
http://www.lycos.com
http://www.mckinley.com
http://www.me.berkeley.edu/ergo
http://www.whowhere.com/wwphone/phone.html
http://www.yahoo.com

A Sample of Successful Search Engine Use

A recent challenge required finding World Wide Web sites that offered guidance on the rescue of pets and livestock from disaster. An efficient use of search engines provided the following references in very little time:

1. Disasters & Your Pet
   http://www.datasync.com/~clpardue/pet.htm

2. Pet Information - Department of Emergency Services in Indian River County, Florida
   http://www.indian-river.fl.us/living/govern/ems/pets.html

3. Humane Society Guidance for Pets and Disasters: Get Prepared
   http://www.saredcross.org/Emergencies/Pets.html

4. Savannah Morning News Tips for Pet Owners: Hurricane 97
   http://www.savanews.com/stories/060197/HURpettips.html

5. American Veterinary Medical Foundation: Grand Forks Disaster Relief
   http://www.avma.org/avmf/gff.htm

6. FEMA: HSUS Urges Pet Owners to Include Pets in Their Hurricane Preparations
   http://www.fema.gov/hu97/hsus03.htm

7. FEMA's Online Library: Animals and Emergencies Room
   http://www.fema.gov/library/lib02.htm

8. FEMA: Through Hell and High Water: Disasters and the Human-Animal Bond
   http://www.fema.gov/home/fema/equine.htm

9. FEMA: The Humane Society of the United State Offers Disaster Planning Tips for Pets, Livestock and Wildlife
   http://www.fema.gov/home/fema/diztips.htm

10. FEMA: Animals and Emergencies
    http://www.fema.gov/fema/anemer.htm

11. FEMA: Reference Library Fact Sheets: Pets and Disasters--Before, During, After
    http://www.fema.gov/fema/petsf.html

12. HSUS Publications
    http://www.hsus.org/pubs.html

13. Chew's Safe a Pet Page
    http://www.teleport.com/~kdrieck/pets/index.html

14. Kyler Laird: Animal Rescue
    http://www.ecn.purdue.edu/~laird/animal_rescue/

15. International Wildlife Education and Conservation "Smile" Newsletter Article, "Include Pets in Fire Safety Programs"
    http://www.aat.org/pethealth.htm

16. MHVNet Rescue Network
    http://rescue.mhv.net/

17. United Animal Nations and Emergency Animal Rescue Service: Northern California Flood Rescue '97
    http://uan-ears.ciexchange.com/flood97/photos.htm

18. United Animal Nations and Emergency Animal Rescue Service home page
   http://uan-ears.ciexchange.com/

19. Why Rescue a Dog
   http://kelvin.marine.usf.edu/~linae/journal/why.html

20. Practice Makes Perfect: An Emergency Animal Rescue Service (EARS) Account of the Northern California Flood by Terri Crisp
   http://www.pathfinder.com/@@ROVacAQALBB4zeyT/PetPath/YYP/special.bottom2.bak.html

&

Master Lists of Emergency Management Sites

Besides this book, there are many other emergency management Web Site compendiums, which can lead you to thousands of additional sources. One of the best is the **Disaster Finder,** which lists hundreds of sites in alphabetical order (not by subject). Simply clicking on a site allows that site to open immediately. The **Disaster Finder** is located at:

http://ltpwww.gsfc.nasa.gov/ndrd/disaster/atod_to.html

Another superb site is the home page for the **Global Emergency Management Service (GEMS),** which contains over 50 categories of emergency management sites at:

http://ltpwww.gsfc.nasa.gov/ndrd/disaster/

FEMA can also keep you updated on new sites of interest in emergency management at:

http://www.fema.gov/fema/whatsnew.htm

To investigate for the latest sites on computer system emergency management you can search for the topic "disaster" at **inquiry.com** found at:

http://www.inquiry.com

If you have an Acrobat™ reader on your computer, and you work with U.S. government agencies, you might consider using the Government Accounting Office guide to 4,300 federal Web sites. It can be found at:

http://www.gao.gov/cgi/bin/getrpt?GGD-97-86s

Push Technology and News Sites

Tools like Domino for Lotus Notes are now available to enhance the Internet experience by reaching out to sample sites for you. All you have to do is visit a review area, not unlike your e-mail box, to find out the latest updates. Contact an Information Technology Specialist to find out what software will work best with your computer system.

You can also keep up with the world and local news through Webcasting software. This allows you to have a news service available on screen—say, in the emergency operations center—when you need it. It can reduce the need to keep scanning television reports of local news as more and more local stations will provide this option. It is now provided mainly by the larger news networks and services that go out and search for specific information periodically. You can read more about this technology is Chapter 10.

A Final Note: Making Peace Through the World Wide Web

One of the challenges in emergency management is peacemaking. There are constant struggles to resolve turf battles and political infighting. There will no doubt be days when no matter how hard you struggle you will have stepped on someone's toes.

Emergency managers and professionals have often asked us, "Isn't there some way I can send a card or greeting on the Internet to soothe some nerves, or maybe just thank a staff member for a job well done." So, we compiled the gift sites we found most useful. All the sites are free, except the florist site. Sometimes you will just have to give in and send real flowers (like the time your boss lost his car in a flood when you gave him the wrong directions to the emergency operations center).

Gift Sites

http://www.virtualpresents.com/
This one has lots of stuff, including cards

http://www.bluemountainarts.com/index.html
I like Blue Mountain. High Quality. Sensitive.

http://www.icecreamusa.com/
Here's a real fun one for sending an ice cream surprise that you concoct via the Web.

http://emedia.commerceasia.com/greeting/
This one is great for seasonal greetings.

http://postcards.www.media.mit.edu/Postcards/
This has one of the largest variety of choices.

To order real flowers:

http://originalsflorist.com/

BRIGHT IDEAS: Play a game of search and find with staff. Ask staff members to find:

✓ a list of Web Site references for a recent topic of concern;

✓ a sample of a UseNet discussion about a specific disaster; and

✓ a new search engine that your staff has not used.

7
Helping Staff Adapt and Adopt

Cultural Change and the Internet

Just knowing how to use a tool is not enough. To make a tool more than a toy, there must be a strategy to bring the tool into everyday use. To allow acceptance. To allow exploration. To allow integration. This chapter is for the emergency managers who have staff with needs for the Internet. It will assist those managers who have not yet introduced the powers of the Internet, or who tried with mixed results. This chapter is also for the managers who are afraid to let the power loose into the hands of staff, or who must justify its use to executive staff or a board.

Change is the new constant. Every emergency management organization in the US has been overwhelmed with wave after wave of upheaval from budget cuts to technological tsunamis. Each new idea is now circumspect. Staff are haggard and tired of the whim-of-the-day club. The Internet may seem initially like a waste of time to many of them. The Internet may appear as another shiny button with no value. Managers are in a similar boat—fighting for every program dollar just to keep staff. It seems ludicrous to battle through the introduction of another idea that staff will complain about bitterly. That is why there is a crucial need for strategy.

Day-to-Day Use

Managers in the 1980s were unhappy with the software manufacturers who installed games on every new computer. Managers were concerned that staff would spend time playing and not working. What the managers did not know was that the manufacturers had a strategy. PC vendors knew that if people played with the computer games they would be drawn to use the computers. And the games were simple enough to be boring after a time. By then, the users had learned many of the basics needed to succeed with other programs. Today's emergency planning managers also need a strategy.

If you use the following strategies, or a similar approach, there will be a much better chance that you will use the Internet as a tool and not an occasional toy. Here is a strategy for careful, planned and efficient cultural change:

30 Days Before Operations

- A month before your Internet service is on line, let staff know about the plan to make it available.

- Make sure they know what kind of training they can receive.

- Let them know how it will be applied to their daily work.

- Let them know the parameters of use.

First Week of Operation

- During the first week of operation, ensure everyone has an e-mail address and is instructed how to send e-mail. Training should include protocols, shorthand, and the use of the e-mail tools your particular software offers.

- Set an objective that everyone must mail out and receive back at least one e-mail from another member of your group.

Second Week of Operations

- The second week's objective should be to send e-mail to an outside agency or organization involved with your group. *Everyone in the group must have proof of this through a printout.*

- For those just beginning (and be careful here not to discriminate against those who already use the Internet) have a series of contests to find certain items, like a scavenger hunt. The first to find all the items at the emergency management Web sites would receive a prize, like a month's subscription to the Internet at their home. That can cost less than $20 out of the office budget—the cheapest training you will ever schedule.

At the End of 30 Days

- Start a users group. There may already be one in a nearby office. Join theirs, or find someone in your group who already has Internet experience. Ask them if they will act as lead to help others.

Two Months

- During the second month, set up a competition to find the most useful new emergency management related Web site. Not only will this intrigue your staff, but it will really get people digging. You will find your base library of Internet references booming. Focus the competition in four areas: preparedness, response, recovery and mitigation. Each category should have its own reward.

Four Months

- By the fourth month, you should be ready to make decisions about having your own Web site. Let everyone on your staff have input to help develop the site. Make sure your staff get a chance to sit in on initial kickoff meetings with the Information Management Specialist.

Six Months

- By month six, begin doing drills with your staff involving disasters that might impact your community, or your jurisdictional boundaries. Let them develop ways they can use the Internet sites they have discovered to enhance your emergency response, recovery, and mitigation.

End of First Year

- By the end of the first year, send a staff member to a conference or outside training on uses of the Internet for emergency management. There should be some available after the publishing of this text.

The PC Challenge: Generation X, Y, and Z

You are about to encounter (if you have not already) the new paradigms of information gathering used by the next generation. The professional group now in their mid-20s and early 30s are not as intensively book and magazine oriented as the generations before them. This group has been dubbed Generation X, unfortunately. For discussion purposes, the authors are going to refer to the baby boomers as Generation Y, and those born prior to WWII as Generation Z.

To infuse your workers with zeal for the Internet, you will need different strategies for the different groups. These rules are generalities, but have been found useful in practical application.

Generation Z

These individuals range from blasé to mortified when it comes to the use of personal computers. Many of them fought the entry of computers into the work place. Most would not even think of having one at home. They have a philosophy of, "I use these things at work. I don't need to bring them into my castle." This group will, in some cases, be the first to complain about the idea of using the Internet. They have seen fancy ideas come and go before, and they are not going to be caught up in the process of another management whim.

Be gentle with these employees. Make sure every one of them gets the full briefing about the changes to come. Be double sure they are supported and stroked for even the slightest accomplishment they make along the lines of use and cooperation. After all, they have one thing the Internet will never have—institutional memory. If they think for one moment that this is one more automation device to run them off the job before retirement...well, you, as a manager, could be in the same realm as General Custer. Make Generation Z a partner in the process. Once you accomplish this, they will be the most avid supporters. They will also ensure Internet access maintenance, which should not be left to Generation X, at any cost.

Generation Y

Generation Y fought in and/or against the Viet Nam War. They have strong opinions, and are the bulwark of the new management styles. Some of them already know more about the Internet than some of your Information Management specialists. The baby boomers of Generation Y have variable computer skill levels based on their personal income and education, but overall they are computer friendly. Generation Y was taught that team playing is the target of excellence. To some degree they believe that. If you introduce the Internet into your office culture through a team integration process, Generation Y will be more likely to cooperate. Also, the Y Generation shares knowledge. Networking is the backbone of their daily operation. They will help Generation Z if one of the Zs gets stuck in computer limbo. Ys are patient enough to work with people who have computer phobias. But, they will demand that everyone in the office have exactly the same advantages of power in software or hardware. This is a generation that requires equity. God help you if you put a better unit on just one person's desk because there was only enough funding to get one upgrade for the office.

What you will find among members of Generation Y is a deep division regarding the name brand of equipment and software. Thus you have IBM camps and MacIntosh camps. There will be those who swear by Microsoft Word™, and those who swear at it as a word processor. Be sure that if this part of your office culture has strong feelings about a hardware or software preference, that you listen and respond to the group input. To place an unwieldy, unwanted tool in front of this group invites lost time, lost morale, and lost productivity. The authors know of more than one case where baby boomers of the Y Generation have left a company after the announcement of a switch from IBM to MacIntosh, or vice versa. Take these preferences seriously, and then let the Ys play with Generation X.

Generation X

There are lots of reasons to stand back and let these employees run with the Internet, like a fish taking the bait. They know what they want, and they want high-tech. They grew up with mice in their teeth and the computer is as comfortable to them as your overstuffed recliner is for you. They don't need the coaxing and prodding. They don't need a sense of team. They just need you to get out of the way.

Some writers once defined this age group as lost, listless, undefined, and not devoted to any cause. That was wrong. They can work as hard as an army of field hands—but they need a reason they choose, not one forced on them. The mores of the previous twentieth century residents mean little to them. They are looking for new horizons. To those in their ranks who already have absorbed the Internet, it is their

Rosetta stone: a source of social and mental solace. They may not want to participate in any of the contests. They definitely will not be patient enough to teach anyone else...unless it makes sense to their plans. But, if you want information off the Internet, and you want it now, they are the winners. Put them on the tough assignments. Hold them in reserve. Don't try to bind wild horses.

Promoting equity

Some of you will not be able to afford a complete, high-tech station for all your staff. What then? With the tightening budgets you need some strategies? There are some alternatives.

✓ Develop a single workstation that can be shared by all of the staff. Set up a schedule so people can sign up for Internet use. Make sure there is a maximum time per user per week. Allow people to trade their time to other users, with the understanding that an individual cannot exceed the total-hours-per-month limit. In this manner, hot projects can be bought for slower hours later in a month.

✓ If there is a budget allowance in your organization for home telework, you may be able to purchase Internet access for the home use of your staff. If not full Internet access, at least access to e-mail. This will have added benefits in distributive location of your staff and in later development of a virtual office and virtual emergency operations center.

✓ If you describe the limitations of the Internet access to your staff, one of your staff may be willing to become the Internet search specialist for all your staff. This will require a change in work assignments and descriptions. It is not the best alternative, although it may be the most practical of answers. Be sure that protocols are in place to ensure that any information the researcher finds is available to all staff. Without this sharing, a single Internet research point will have little value.

✓ Last, there is one oddity. It is an unusual answer that a few businesses and organizations have tried. You can search out an office nearby that has access to your office that would be willing to share their Internet accessibility. You can exchange something else of value with them to ensure there is a quid pro quo. Some have shared copiers for heavy work projects. Some have shared parking spaces. Others offer to share extra office space when there is an overflow day for an office that practices hoteling. There have been successes and failures with this methodology. It may be an answer for you. Caveat emptor.

Training: The Final Frontier

There are no alternatives for quality training for your staff and you. Self-motivation can only go so far. To provide the best possible outcomes for Internet use, arrange for professional staff training. This training will be most effective if you can send the entire staff at the same time to a facility that allows hands-on experience.

The next choice is sending your best support person (a Y Generation member) to pick up the training and bringing it back to everyone else. This assignment needs to be clearly defined before that person is sent, however. Your representative will take better notes knowing the expectation is to train the rest of your staff.

Another choice is buying support tapes and letting staff learn the finer points on their own time and as they feel motivated. Do not anticipate a strong result from this ploy. It costs less, and there is a reason.

Access Control

 One of the key concerns of office management is access control to sensitive systems. This concern has spread to management of the Internet. Managers are concerned about inappropriate surfing and improper messages being sent by e-mail. Each office is different in its restraints, but the authors believe it is best to leave a system as open as possible when users are learning a new computer tool. If it is absolutely necessary to control where staff can visit on the Web, consider using software that can isolate those sites. If you have a nation-wide ISP, like America Online, they usually offer a service that will lock out certain sites at your request. Some security software allows even broader restriction in terms of other Internet forums (FTP, IRC, etc.).

The authors recommend using any one of the following software programs:

- Cyber Patrol™

- CyberSitter™

- Net Nanny™

- SurfWatch™

- Time's Up

Of course, most of the programs can be bypassed by clever computer users. But for beginners, it can be an effective tool to screen abusive activity. To keep up with some of the latest try at the site set up by *Connect-Time Magazine* at: http://www.connect-time.com/tutorials/blockers.html

Security

You may want to restrict access to the Internet server. If you are in an office shared by several departments, this may be necessary. To control access, simply restrict it through your platform, such as Windows 95/NT™ and Novell™.

Viruses

There is always a risk that your staff may bring a virus into your system if they do not take appropriate care. Here are some simple rules you should share with staff:

- Do not load executable files (files that end in .exe).

- Do not accept programs that are offered by prompts that were not requested.

- Close the choice on your Web browser that allows Java script connection [translation] .

- Use a virus check software.

To keep your system clear, use a virus checking software that is regularly updated. This software should be used every time the computer is started, and after every use of the Internet. That takes a great deal of discipline on the part of you and your staff. It is critical, however, in an age of pranksters. The authors recommend any of the following anti-virus softwares:

- Norton™

- McAfee™

is added separately from planning because it is a precursor to the planning process. It is becoming a regular part of the daily operations activities in emergency management.

These approaches may not be the only viable answers. For instance, you may notice that some sites are repeated as resources in almost every scenario. That is because those sites have proven to be dependable resources for information in almost all situations. However, you may develop a completely different approach to address the scenarios. That is completely acceptable and reasonable within the range of management skills and preferences.

Please also keep in mind that the Internet is neither a substitute for experience and skills in emergency management, nor a public library. The Web sites and other sources will merely enhance the abilities emergency management staff already have and use. These choices are presented as a rough blue print for efficient and thorough information gathering when the test scenarios occur, and:

- You are the only person available to perform research;

- Your time is limited;

- You have limited research materials in your office or limited public library access; and

- You need the most up-to-date resources available.

Scenarios

Here are the basic scenarios. Our answers will follow. Try to work through each one without reading ahead, if you can.

1.	**Planning:**	You have been asked to prepare a plan dealing with medical response for a large-scale terrorist attack. What Internet sources could you use in your research project?
2.	**Response:**	You are in the middle of response coordination for a major flood. You need some suggestions for advanced planning in anticipation of a major surge expected in 48 hours? What Internet sites might provide some ideas or information?

3.   **Relief:**   You are expecting an onslaught of relief needs for those caught in a major disaster. What Internet resources be of value in preparing an effective campaign?

4.   **Recovery:**   You expect to incur billions of dollars of response losses from a natural disaster. What Internet sources could assist you in your recovery strategy planning?

5.   **Mitigation:**   You are requested to work with local officials to change building codes and zoning based on flood zone maps. What Internet resources might be useful in the process?

6.   **Research:**   You are asked to search for current federal laws, regulations, and proposed legislation that may impact your emergency management program. Where can you look on the Internet?

We have just served you a platter of goodies. But, there is no peeking! Give each one a try. Work on these slowly. Try one a day, or a week if you don't have more time. Write down your answers and then check them against our answers on the following pages.

Good hunting!

Answers

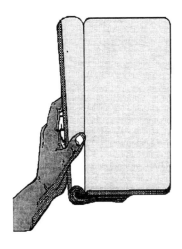

1.   Planning

You have been asked to prepare a plan dealing with medical response for a large-scale terrorist attack. What Internet sources could you use in your research project?

Approach: Break the topic down into its integral subject areas in Chapter 3 which are planning, health/medical considerations, and terrorism. Planning information might also be found in listings under the category of general topics in Chapter 3, since planning is a general topic area.

The basic Internet sites and associated tools the authors would utilize are:

Planning

- The FEMA site featuring the *State and Local Guide for All Hazards Emergency Operations Planning*

Medical

- The Center for Disaster Education and Research's MedicCom Bulletin Board
- The Center for Disease Control in Atlanta
- The Medicine and Global Survival Magazine
- The Global Health Disaster Network home page

Terrorism

- Counter Intelligence and Counter Terrorism home page
- Yahoo Terrorism Search Page
- Counter -Terrorism home page
- Terrorist Group Profiles pages
- Edgewood Enterprise home page

Additional Sites to Consider

- DMAT sites
- FEMA
- SALEMDUG
- NEMA
- NCCEM
- Natural Hazards Research Center
- *Stonefly* Newsletter
- LISTSERV
- Newsgroup
- Search engines looking for terrorism planning, medical planning, hospital planning, etc.
- E-mail to state emergency agency planning offices and personal contacts

Printed References

- *Safety and Health on the Internet*, by Ralph B. Stuart, III, for listings
- *Chemical Guide to the Internet*, by C.C. Lee, for listings
- *Emergency Planning and Management*, by William H. Stringfield, for structure

2. Response

You are in the middle of response coordination for a major flood. You need some suggestions for advanced planning in anticipation of a major surge which is expected in 48 hours? What Internet sites might provide some ideas or information?

Approach: Break the topic down into its integral subject areas which are flood and preparedness. Preparedness information might also be found under the category of general topics in Chapter 3, since preparedness is a general topic area.

Preparedness

- The FEMA site featuring the *State and Local Guide for All Hazards Emergency Operations Planning*

Flood

The basic Internet sites and associated tools the authors would utilize are:

- Your state's conservation board, department of water resources, or natural resources department
- Public water utilities in your state that have Web sites
- U. S. Bureau of Reclamation home page
- U.S. Corps of Engineers home page
- U.S. Geological Survey site for reporting stream flows
- U.S. Geological Survey site for Water Resources of the United States
- Federal Energy Regulatory Commission home page
- Dartmouth College Global Flood Monitoring home page
- State emergency agencies, with home pages, that have responded to floods

Additional Sites to Consider

- FEMA
- SALEMDUG
- NEMA
- NCCEM
- Natural Hazards Research Center
- *Stonefly* newsletter
- LISTSERV
- Newsgroup
- Search engines under floods, flooding, flood plain management, flood planning
- E-mail to state emergency agency planning offices(specifically a state that has had major flooding in the last year), and personal contacts

Printed References

- Emergency Planning Guidance (see *Emergency Planning and Management*, by William H. Stringfield, for structure)

3. Relief

You are expecting an onslaught of relief needs for those caught in a major disaster. What Internet resources may be of value in preparing an effective campaign?

Approach: Break the topic down into its integral subject areas which are preparedness and relief. Under those main topics, you should search the Web Sites for information about mass feeding, mental health, and community-based organizations.

Preparedness

- The FEMA site featuring the *State and Local Guide for All Hazards Emergency Operations Planning*
- American Red Cross

Care and Shelter

- American Red Cross
- International Committee of the Red Cross home page
- Salvation Army
- National Guard in your state
- Water vendors
- Portable toilet vendors

Mass Feeding

- American Red Cross
- International Committee of the Red Cross home page
- Salvation Army
- National Guard in your state
- Portable kitchens and food purveyors

Mental Health

- Mass Emergencies Project home page
- Your state's social services agency home page
- County offices in the affected regions, via their home page
- Hospitals in the affected region

Community Based Organizations

- National Voluntary Organizations Active in Disaster (NVOAD)
- National Emergency Resource Information Network (NERIN)

Additional Sites to Consider

- Relief Now home page
- Center of Excellence in Disaster Management and Humanitarian Assistance
- International Emergency and Refugee Health Programs home page
- UN Department of Humanitarian Affairs
- Other states that have had recent large relief efforts
- FEMA (especially areas on relief, and mass care and shelter)
- SALEMDUG
- NEMA
- NCCEM
- Natural Hazards Research Center
- *Stonefly* newsletter
- LISTSERV
- Newsgroup
- Search engines on relief, mass care and shelter, and mental health
- E-mail to state emergency agency planning offices and personal contacts who have recently been involved in relief operations

Printed References

- *Emergency Planning and Management*, William H. Stringfield
- *Disaster Assistance: A Guide to Recovery Programs*, FEMA 229(4), November, 1995
- *Disaster Cost Recovery Guidelines: Recovering Costs for Building Damage or Loss and Seeking Payment for Increased Services*, Alameda County Card Project, 1996

4.   Recovery

You expect to incur billions of dollars of response losses from a natural disaster.   What Internet sources could assist you in your recovery strategy planning?

Approach: Break the topic down into its integral subject areas which are preparedness and recovery.   Financial recovery information may be found in listings under general topics in Chapter 3, since recovery is a general topic area.

Preparedness

- The FEMA site featuring the *State and Local Guide for All Hazards Emergency Operations.*

Recovery

- FEMA (recovery areas)
- States with recent cost recovery experience (use one of the larger states—California or Florida)
- University of Illinois Cooperative Extension Service Disaster Services home page
- California State Governor's Office of Emergency Services home page
- SALEMDUG
- NEMA
- NCCEM
- Natural Hazards Research Center
- *Stonefly* newsletter
- LISTSERV
- Newsgroup
- Search engines for recovery activities
- E-mail to state emergency agency planning offices and personal contacts

5.   Mitigation

You are requested to work with local officials to change building codes and zoning based on flood zone maps. What Internet resources might be useful in the process?

Approach: Break the topic down into its integral subject areas which are preparedness and mitigation. Mitigation information might also be found in any listing under the category of general topics in Chapter 3, since mitigation is a general topic area. Also note the answers to scenario 6: Research. There are many new laws regarding mitigation. It may be of value to use the research techniques in the answers to scenario 6.

Preparedness

- The FEMA site featuring the *State and Local Guide for All Hazards Emergency Operations.*

Mitigation

- FEMA (Mitigation sites, which are numerous)
- FEMA (National Flood Insurance Program sites, which are numerous)
- FEMA (Hazard Mitigation Grant Program)
- U.S. Geological Survey
- International Multi-Hazard Mitigation Partnership
- U.S Government Accounting Office
- U.S. Government Printing Office
- Insurance Institute for Property Loss Reduction
- American Risk and Insurance Association
- Council of State Governments or National League of Cities
- International Center for Disaster Mitigation Engineering
- International Decade for Natural Disaster Reduction site for mitigation discussion
- U.S. Chamber of Commerce
- Builder's Associations (e.g., ATC or International Conference of Building Officials)
- Other states with communities with recent flood mitigation efforts (use one of the larger states—California or Florida)

- SALEMDUG
- NEMA
- NCCEM
- Natural Hazards Research Center
- *Stonefly* newsletter
- LISTSERV
- Newsgroup
- Search engines
- E-mail to state emergency agency planning offices and personal contacts

Printed References

- *Emergency Planning and Management*, William H. Stringfield
- *Disaster Assistance: A Guide to Recovery Programs*, FEMA 229(4), November 1995
- *Disaster Cost Recovery Guidelines: Recovering Costs for Building Damage or Loss and Seeking Payment for Increased Services*, Alameda County Card Project, 1996

6. **Research**

You are asked to search for current federal laws, regulations, and proposed legislation that may impact your emergency management program. Where can you look on the Internet?

Approach: Break the topic down into its integral subject areas which are preparedness and laws/regulations. Regulation and proposed legislation might also be found in any of the listings in Chapter 3, since these topics are of general interest to most emergency managers. Check the laws/regs box for each site.

NOTE: A number of places on the Internet offer free access to such references as the Code of Federal Regulations. Although the access is free, it is our experience that the postings are sometimes outdated and inaccurate. It is better, if you are in a critical role of regulatory oversight, to pay a vendor on the Internet who is responsible for updating critical references such as regulations and case law.

Preparedness

- The FEMA site featuring the *State and Local Guide for All Hazards Emergency Operations.*
- Other state sites that have state emergency plan legal references listed.

Pending Legislation

- State legislatures on the Web (almost all state legislatures now have a site capable of access by the public to track bills)
- Federal legislation sites

Laws

- Find Law
- Nexus-Lexus
- West Publishing: Westlaw
- Check your state to see if it has placed all of its laws on the Internet

Regulations

- Regulations on the Web
- Counterpoint Publishing
- Check your state to see if it has placed all of its regulations on the Internet

Additional Sites to Consider

- GALE Net
- Library of Congress
- Government Accounting Office
- Government Printing Office
- Research-it home page
- FEMA (legislation and regulation section)
- Council of State Governments or National League of Cities
- SALEMDUG (legislation and regulation section)
- NEMA
- NCCEM
- Natural Hazards Research Center
- *Stonefly* newsletter
- LISTSERV
- Newsgroup
- Search engines
- E-mail to state emergency agency planning offices and personal contacts

Printed References

- *Safety and Health on the Internet*, by Ralph B. Stuart, III, for listings
- *Chemical Guide to the Internet*, by C.C. Lee, for listings
- *Emergency Planning and Management*, by William H. Stringfield, for structure
- *Environmental Guide to the Internet*, by Carol Briggs-Erickson and Toni Murphy
- *Recycling and Waste Management Guide to the Internet*, by Roger M. Guttentag, for listings

Bright Ideas:

Play "what-if" scenarios with your staff to develop their Internet skills. Ask staff members to consider:

✓ finding new sites to meet an anticipated seasonal challenge (flooding, tornadoes etc.);

✓ E-mailing other Internet users in emergency management for hot sites they have found useful; and

✓ evaluating software that will automatically survey sites by topic for use in the emergency operations center during disaster response.

9
Building Your Own Web Site

The Good, The Bad, the ...

After six months of exposure to other Web Sites, you may want a site of your own. Congratulations! By sharing your organization's information and expertise you will aid the advancement of emergency management worldwide. You may not believe your site could do this, but you have already experienced what other sites can do for you. The developers of the sites you have viewed never knew you were coming. Those developers might have established their site for some other purpose. Imagine how many serendipitous meetings might be ahead after you put your shingle on the Internet.

Not everyone was thrilled when the database *Tobin Surfs the Net* was first released. Some emergency management site Web masters were less than thrilled by what was termed a "caustic and arbitrary" rating system. The fact is, there are still many sites today that seem to go out of their way to make the reader work to find the information. Internet readers do not have time for these antics. To help you avoid being placed in the group of low performance sites, the authors have provided this thumbnail sketch of how to avoid the perils of poor site design.

Don't Start in a Vacuum

Before you start thinking "outside of the box", do not forget who else is in the box with you. As the emergency manager, you'll have a certain perspective about what message you want to deliver. However, you should involve all your staff to make sure their interests are also considered. You'll also get more support if you ask your critical audience for input before designing the site.

Other key players in your organization may need inclusion as well, such as:

- Information Management Specialists

- Public Information Officer

- Human Resources Officer

- GIS Specialists

- Agency Webmaster

- Administrative Support

Basic Components

There are four basic structural components you will need to build your site:

1. An Internet Services Provider (previously discussed in Chapter 2)

2. Software to design the site layout and content

3. Quality graphics and design elements, including photos and maps

4. E-mail capacity for reader queries

Training Comes First

Do your homework before you decide how to develop your site. For the beginner, the authors would recommend attending at least one course in Hypertext Markup Language (**HTML**) before selecting a site-design software package. These courses are offered by many local training schools and specialty community training centers, as well as by vendors traveling throughout the country. This exposure will let you explore the types of software you need based on your interests and the level of expertise you want to develop. If you and your staff want to learn how to build a Web Site through remote learning on the Internet, consider visiting the McGraw-Hill World

University. Their courses cover all the basic and advanced techniques you will need. Their Web Site is:

http://www.mhcec.com

Software Choices

There are many software packages available to assist you with a Web Site and home page design. These programs range in price from under $100 to almost $1000. When it is time to select a site development software package, the authors recommend considering one of the following:

- FrontPage (Microsoft Corporation)

- HotDog Pro (Sausage Software Ltd.)

- HotMetal (SoftQuad Corp.)

However, you may already have some Web Site authoring tools already on your computer if you own one of the following office suites:

- Corel WordPerfect Suite

- Microsoft Office

- Lotus SmartSuite

To ensure that your Web Site meets all legal requirements, such as copyright and intellectual property, make sure you obtain a copy of *Creating a Web Site: A Preventive Law Guide,* which is available from Assets Protection Publishing, P.O. Box 5323, Madison, Wisconsin 53705-0323.

Graphics

Yes, a picture is worth a thousand words, but a photo, fancy diagram or animated character may take too much time to load for those with slower systems. If necessary, use graphics sparingly and where they will have the most impact,. There are many sites on the Internet that provide all of the free graphics imaginable. Your development software package will also offer some. The authors recommend you consider using graphics already available to save money and time. Designing your own graphics may be distinctive, but if you don't have the skills yourself, homemade ideas can—well, stink, actually. Look at what other sites have done that you like and consider what is best for your message and your subject area. Remember your audience. Speed is second only to content. Flash will not bring people back.

Scanning graphics can be costly. Your organization may already have the capability to produce high-quality scanned images if you have a monthly newsletter or magazine. If you do not have access and you go to a vendor for this service, shop wisely. There are wide variances in price for virtually the same quality of product. But, there are also plenty of free graphics available without fees for copyright use, that are readily available on the Internet. Just copy them from the graphic sites onto your web page. The authors suggest you try some of these graphic art sites:

- My Animated GIF Collection Part II (http://www.joed.com/animated/)

- Barry's Clip Art Server (http://www.barrysclipart.com/)

- Yahoo Guide to Internet Icons
  (http://www.yahoo.com/Computers/World_Wide_Web/Programming/Icons/)

E-mail

The use of e-mail is a valuable element of your site. The ability and desire to be contacted by other interested emergency management professionals will garner many rewards. The networking that can occur in this manner can open new vistas and opportunities for your program. In addition, it fulfills each emergency manager's professional responsibility to assist others in the field.

The only major questions regarding e-mail connections to your Web Site are 1) should it be an e-mail address separate from your daily use e-mail, and 2) what software works best if you are just selecting an e-mail product.

From experience, the authors recommend trying your regular e-mail address in the beginning to establish the volume of traffic coming to the site. Monitor the site for about a month. If you are getting more than 20 inquiries a day, you might think of going to a separate e-mail address. If you plan to have critical information posted during disasters that affect your organization's jurisdiction or territory, you will definitely need to have a separate address.

There are dozens of quality e-mail software packages available. You may already have an e-mail tool in your primary software suite or web browser. Many people use these built-in tools effectively. Stand alone programs that the authors recommend include:

- Eudora Pro (Qualcomm)

- cc:Mail (Lotus)

Cost

If you do not feel you have the skills to design a Web Site yourself, then consider hiring a vendor. Depending on the design requirements for your site, you could spend hundreds or thousands of dollars for someone else's assistance. Paying more than $500 to build a basic home page and Web Site structure is probably a poor use of funds for most emergency management programs. If the vendor wants more, visit other vendors, or better yet, work with your Information Management Specialist.

There is a plethora of web design vendors. You can find them through local advertisements in computer magazines, through computer clubs, and through the hundreds listed on the Internet after a basic search with any search engine tool. The authors will not recommend any specific vendor due to the liabilities involved. If you like a site you've found on the Internet, query the Webmaster and ask if they used a vendor. If you finally decide to approach a vendor, you should do the following:

- Find out the vendor's experience, obtain his/her time in business and a client list.

- Look at the vendor's client's home pages.

- Get an estimate for a basic home page and for each additional feature.

- Establish whether or not there are any production restrictions. If they have a low price, but it takes a year to get the final product, the vendor may not be a bargain.

- Establish what it will cost for modifications and upgrades.

- Obtain at least six estimates (you will be surprised at the range of prices).

You can also experiment at no cost whatsoever, and spend very little time, to see what a basic site might look like with your information. WebSpawner™ offers such a service with the hope that users will want to try enhanced features that make the site more useful and attractive. This vendor's site and services are worth considering. This approach may be the cheapest for your needs. Check them out at:
http://www.webspawner.com/

There may also be other costs if your organization does not own its own Internet server. The ISP your organization uses for e-mail may charge a monthly fee for the space on their server hard drive. The ISP may also charge extra if your site has a large number of visits, known as "hits." Hits tie up an ISP server time, and may impact the ISP's capacity for their commercial customers. You will also find that ISP vendors vary in how they offer space. Some allow Web Site space and time as part of an existing customer's monthly fee base. Be sure to shop ISP Web Site vendors just like design vendors.

Maintenance

It is important to keep your site maintained. If you don't keep your site up-to-date, few people will visit and the information you have installed will quickly drift from out-of-date to misinformation. It is best to consider staff costs for information updates. Dedicated staffing is the missing link for a successful Web Site. If management cannot identify and commit staff resources to keep the site timely and attractive, then it may be best not to have a Web Site.

A rule of thumb is to allow one staff day a month to update and maintain a single Web Site once it has been established. This maintenance includes:

- Updating hot links

- Evaluating traffic (hits)

- Adding new material or updating old

- Redesigning weak areas

- Answering e-mail inquiries

- Developing new capacities as required, such as voice, video, or white-boarding

- Staff briefings/training on use of the Web Site

What Works Best for a Web Site

There are many texts available for designing a Web Site. Here are some specific points to consider that will make your emergency management site more effective, based on our experience in emergency management and after using hundreds of Internet sites that focus on emergency management issues.

✓ Keep text large—at least 14 point font. Too many sites use a smaller font size to save space. Baby-boomers (Y Generation) may think this is not necessary. Mature users (Z Generation) may think the idea irritating, since they believe this means they have to get special treatment because they are older. The fact is that bifocals can put a severe strain on the eyes of power users who like to surf Web Sites. And please stick to one style of font. Constantly switching font styles may seem artistic, but it is inefficient for transferring data.

✓ Use graphics sparingly. They slow down the loading process. Many users have slower modems and browsing software. Their computer systems may hang up when they access a Web Site with intricate or complex graphic designs. However, it is certainly wise to have a section with graphics and photos separate from the main text. Use a menu selection button so the readers who want to load those items can have separate access. It is also wise to add an option at the prompt, when your site first appears on the screen, that allows the visitor to shut off graphics, if they so desire.

✓ Keep the concepts short, simple and avoid long paragraphs. If you have a large base of information, such as a large database or huge tables, consider providing a location where the reader can download this material as a separate file (hopefully in a compressed format, like PKZIP™). You might also speed the reader's capacity to find what they need from your data by installing a search engine for your site that will look for specific subjects of interest.

✓ Keep the site updated. Let the reader know on the first page when the last update occurred so they will know if there has been a recent update or a change since they last visited. The prompt should say something like, "This site was last updated on _____".

✓ Use hot-link bullets that the reader can select to visit related sites. However, if you don't check these connections every six months, these buttons will soon become useless and frustrating to the visitors.

✓ If you use a graphic background for your text, keep it simple and pastel or passive. Too many sites have tried to provide exciting backgrounds that make the text difficult to read and complicate printing. If you want to protect the script from direct printing, then consider using white script on a dark background.

✓ Provide an e-mail tool on the home page so visitors will have direct access to the Webmaster or key contact for your organization.

✓ Ensure that each page has a reference block that allows the reader to return to the home page and/or the main menu section.

What to Avoid When Designing a Web Site

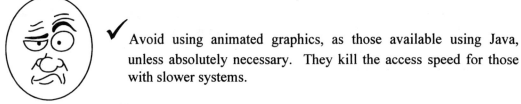

✓ Avoid using animated graphics, as those available using Java, unless absolutely necessary. They kill the access speed for those with slower systems.

✓ Avoid hot-links to sites that are not related to your message. Many sites try to become a focus for almost every activity imaginable. This often dilutes the primary message they convey. The authors have also found that these sites are often poorly maintained because there is simply too much information to keep updated. Focus on what your organization does best. Include links that enhance your message.

✓ Avoid surprises. If you know your site will be unavailable to the general public during disasters, say so on the home page. If you know your site will be down for maintenance, or you are changing servers and URL codes, let the readers know. It is considered very rude netiquette to change locations and not leave a forwarding message at the old server site.

Normal vs. Disaster Operations

Disaster information is a hot topic—even with the general public. This is a blessing and a curse. Emergency managers need to consider this carefully when developing the contents of a Web Site. If the Web Site has none of the following contents, there may not be a need for special security considerations during disaster operations:

- Secure information (e.g., critical facility maps, diagrams of secured facilities)

- Privacy Act information (e.g., home phone numbers and addresses)

- Emergency operations center functions (e.g., chat areas, e-mail, sensitive GIS maps)

- Status boards or inter-agency communications used during disaster operations

If your Web Site meets any of these criteria, consider some of the following security countermeasures:

- Disable the Web Site access to everyone during disasters. You may have to do this to ensure that the site server is not overwhelmed. (Discuss this with your ISP vendor before opening the site.)

- Transfer the "sensitive materials" areas to another, secured section of the server, so that only those with specific access codes can reach it. This allows the general public to continue to access the Web Site if there are specific types of information your organization still wants to post publicly during the disaster operations.

- Establish a **mirror** Web Site that is activated solely for disaster operations. Only organizations with pre-designated codes would have access.

- Develop a firewall to reduce the effects of tampering by "hackers." A firewall is a protective device provided by software installed by the ISP vendor and/or the Web Site designer. Hackers are individuals who are motivated to disrupt or disable the operation of computer site, their software, or systems. Government and big-business Web Sites have been the primary targets for this tampering.

You can find out more about protecting your site by investigating these software vendors:

- Border Network Technologies

- Ingress

- Raptor

Bad Things Sometimes Happen

A prime example of why protection is critical occurred during the 1997 floods in California. One state agency used a Web Site for displaying data from selected stream flow gauges on some Northern California rivers. Unfortunately, this was a public access site. The information was valuable for planning for resources management and flooding impact potentials. The site was overwhelmed by hits from the public and media. The ISP server was first slowed, then crashed from the overload. The Web Site was lost during one of the most active periods of stream flow monitoring. Limited security protections were installed because public interest volume was not anticipated. A mirror site could have prevented this loss. A mirror site allows alternate access without impacting the home page server. Emergency managers should anticipate that their sites may receive heavy traffic during major disaster situations due to the increased interest from the public.

As noted in Chapter 10, recent experiences by FEMA and state governments indicate that any Web Site that provides information about a disaster in progress will receive tremendous attention, especially if the event is:

- Newsworthy and has generated media attention;

- Large in scope and impact;

- At a well known landmark or key tourism location; and

- At the scene of a major public event, (e.g., a major sporting event, political event, celebration, entertainment site)

One Other Alternative for Carrying Out the Message

When a disaster strikes, you might find other sites on which to piggy-back your message. If your organization is not well known in the community, or has not developed public acknowledgment as an authority for emergency management information, you should find out who is and coordinate with them for joint news releases on their Web Site.

You may also be approached by other organizations because your organization is the recognized messenger of choice. Before you accept this role, ask the requester the following questions:

1. Will they provide staff to assist with placement of information on the Web Site?

2. How much information is to be added?

3. How often will information need to be updated?

4. Who approves the information?

5. Do you get review and approval privileges (this is a must)?

6. Do they only want a hot-link button to their site added to your site?

7. Has their material been virus checked before being transmitted?

8. Can a working site be established prior to a disaster so that new information is merely plugged into a skeleton place holder until it is needed?

Bright Ideas: Coordinate your Web Site design with your staff. Ask your staff to help by:

✓ selecting the best-designed emergency management Web Site,

✓ selecting the elements they feel are critical; and

✓ writing the critical text to enter into the home page.

10
The Future of Emergency Management on the Internet

Not Just a Crystal Ball

The authors hope to offer you an insight into what might happen when you use the Internet for emergency management, and how to apply this knowledge to your advantage. Changes will be coming fast and furious. Keep this chapter in mind and you will be ready for the coming changes.

There are three things that will shape the future regarding the use of the Internet: the World Wide Web, the hardware configurations for transporting information, and the skill of the users. Much of this chapter is devoted to the Internet and hardware "toys," but the essential element will always be the people factor. No matter how carefully a new technology is crafted, without a strategy for user interface, the technology may become a burden rather than an aid. One of the concerns the authors have is that technologies will just be piled on in the work place, rather than integrated. That is why we wrote Chapter 7. Whatever steps you take as the future unfolds, remember that skilled people must be at the other side of the screen for this brave new tool to work. Do not forget to invest in training, drills and exercises. Technology will aid your efforts in emergency management, but only trained personnel will save your program.

If You Are Not Convinced

The World Wide Web is so hot that during the Oklahoma Bombing investigation a site devoted to tips and information on suspects had 27,000 visits in just two days. That is the power of the Internet. If you still think that the use of the World Wide Web

234 / Emergency Planning on the Internet

is an anomaly, just consider the use of Web Sites during the 1997 flooding along the Red River. This flood affected Minnesota, North Dakota and Manitoba, Canada. There was enough interest from the emergency management community, the public and the media to generate massive Internet activity. North Dakota flooding was covered by many World Wide Web Sites, including:

http://www.nacec.org/
http://www.ndsu.nodak.edu/fargoflood/
http://www.northscape.com/news/floodwatch.htm
http://www.pioneerplanet.com/
http://www.pptv.org/floodcam
http://www.whatshotin.com/Features/features32fargo.shtml
http://www.yahoo.com/News_and_Media/Current_Events/Flood_in_the_Plains/

The following Web Sites were for just for Manitoba:

http://www.gov.mb.ca/flood
http://www.gov.mb.ca/gs/memo/index.html
http://www.manflood.com/
http://www.mb.ec.gc.ca/flood/
http://www.mbnet.mb.ca/city/html/govern/water/dyke.htm
http://www.mbnet.mb.ca/city/html/govern/water/flood.htm
http://www.mbnet.mb.ca/floodzone/
http://www.ndsu.nodak.edu/fargoflood/ff_jhu.htm
http://www.netreader.com/flood/
http://www.redcross.ca/e/floods97.html
http://www.umanitoba.ca/news/flood97/
http://www.wpgbiz.net/flood/

FEMA also has experienced the power of the Internet in the last few years. The best example is the incredible increase in visits to their hurricane Web Site:

- Hurricane Opal, 1995—225,000 visits a week

- Hurricane Bertha, 1996—1.5 million visits a week

- Hurricane Fran, 1996—400,000 visits in just one day

You would have to be completely out of touch not to get the picture. The World Wide Web is changing how to plan, communicate and relate with the public, as well as management and staff. Here are just a few of the recent examples how governments have used the World Wide Web:

- West Virginia developed a Geographic Information Systems Public Empowerment Project that allows access to GIS information through the Internet for government and the public;

- Orange County, Florida developed a site, using Army technology, to assist local emergency management in its planning and exercise operations; and

- New York State Library built a repository of GIS maps in a Web Site to be used as a clearinghouse for anyone wanting the information.

People, People Who Need People

There are a million ways to say help in English, and very few words that say how to give or accept it. This section will discuss some new items on the market that can help you and your staff bring your people skills up to par with the Internet changes. One of the biggest concerns is what some have called the reversed Middle Ages of data management, when futurists had hoped for an information renaissance. Unlike during the Middle Ages, there is a glut of information, not a lack. But people are reacting similarly. People want to know less as technologies race ahead and data overwhelms an already busy day. The dizzying changes have driven some people away from the brave new tool. They want to hole up in a cave where they will not be assaulted with anymore information glut. The truth is that it is not the product but the process that is overwhelming users. This is a need that must be addressed, and soon.

First, there is the problem of how to increase the information processing. One company is attempting to address that problem. Imagine doubling your reading capacity? You might just be able to do that with Cornix Java, software that allows a skimming of Web Sites. Its designers, the people of Tenax Software Engineering, claim that a person can learn to move through text at over 1000 words per minute. Now that is doing more with less! Evelyn Woods, eat your heart out.

Second, there is outright fear. Technophobia was touched on in Chapter 7. How real is it? One recent study found that forty percent of people absolutely resist new technologies, especially computers. When thirty percent of managers who attend computer classes still feel threatened after the classes, what is happening? This means you must develop a better strategy in the work place. Without a staggered, pleasant integration, the Internet may be a source of stress and work turmoil. Investigate the work of Michelle Weil in the brochure she developed with MCI. It is free by just calling (800) 779-0000. Ask for *Techno-Therapy: A Guide to Overcoming Your Communications Fears.* Ms. Weils' work is also featured at http://www.ocpapsych.com/weil.htm.

Third, there is the need for increased access to education. Luckily, your staff might not even have to leave the office anymore to get a decent, useful training class, and even a degree. Many universities and colleges are forging ahead with "virtual training classes" via the Internet. One of the leaders in this area in the McGraw-Hill World University. You should investigate the types of courses they offer at www.mhcec.com to get an idea of what will soon be widely available. FEMA has plans to offer an entire series of courses through the Internet. FEMA is completely aware of the declining budgets for travel associated with training, even when the Agency supplements the training costs for government employees. The Internet is becoming the place to learn and meet others who are open-minded to new frontiers.

Realizing Your Own Knowledge

Before continuing on to the software and hardware discussions, take a deep breath. Relax. Do not be intimidated by the acronyms and numbers. The authors have heard some wild stories in the last few years about people who had no computer skills whatsoever. You can consider yourself beyond those who:

- Were angry that the computer did nothing for two days after they received it—even though it was unplugged;

- Were angry because the foot pedal didn't work—they thought the mouse was a treadle like a sewing machine foot control;

- Were angry at service representatives when they were asked if they had read the manual—why should they when they just paid thousands for a computer?; and

- Faxed a photocopy of their floppy to the manufacturer when they were asked to send a copy of their disk.

Everyone starts somewhere. You might laugh at the true examples given above, but all of us were at that stage at one time or another. Allow yourself the space to grow into the ideas presented next. They might take a little time to absorb. Take your time. Investigate. Ponder. Don't try to get it all at once. It is the future, so you have time.

Words to the Wise: An Acronym/Definition List

Normally acronym and definition lists would be found at the back of the book, but this chapter is so specialized we felt it belonged here. You will need it to thread your way through the technical discussions, and in your conversations with your Internet Service Provider, your public switched network provider (phone company) and your Information Management specialist.

ADSL	Asymmetric Digital Subscriber Line
ATM	Asynchronous Transfer Mode (a method of transferring tremendous amounts of data across the Internet system)
DC	Digital Camera
DVC	Digital Video Camcorder
DVC	Desktop Videoconferencing
GIS	Geographic Information System
GPS	Global Positioning System
H.323	A standard for DVC
ISDN	Integrated Services Digital Network
LAN	Local Area Network
Mbps	Megabits per second
MMDS	Multi-channel Multi-point Distribution Service (a method for connecting cable TV distribution to wireless operations
RADSL	Rate Adaptive Digital Subscriber Line
Scalable	A system that will search for and use the highest rate of data transmission available on whatever type of communications line it is connected.
T1	A fiber optic line rating indicating a bandwidth of 1.544 megabits per second

T2	A phone line that handles very large volumes of data, @ 45 megabits per second capacity
T3	A fiber optic line rating indicating a bandwidth of 45 megabits per second
VDSL	Very-high bit rate Digital Subscriber Line, for modems in the 52 megabits per second range
WAN	Wide Area Network
WDM	Wavelength Division Multiplexing (a method to speed transmission speeds)

Software Advances

Browsers Change

It is unclear whether browsers, such as Netscape™, are headed in a direction which will harm or assist emergency management's use of the Internet. The trend seems to be to build a browser that not only manipulates the Internet, but also attempts to manipulate your entire PC and perhaps your entire office intranet. Be careful how the darker side of this new all-in-one backbone technology impacts your operations. The newer versions of browsers will also offer collaborative tools such as white boarding, video/audio conferencing, chat capabilities, and file exchange. In any case, expect the Internet browsers to take up more space and possibly slow your systems. Stick with an older form and don't upgrade if the software becomes too burdensome for your server or PC.

One of the newest tools in the browsers is sampling. Samplers allow you to designate which Web Sites you would like to visit and over what period to time. The sampler collects the latest data and compiles it at one site to allow immediate access. What does this mean for your operation? When your emergency operations center (**EOC**) is open, your response staff will not have to struggle with constantly going back and forth between Internet addresses to get the latest information. The browser's sampler will have done this already. California's State Office of Emergency Services is installing this application using the Lotus Domino™ software.

There are a host of other Internet information providers that search for key information, much of which is valuable to emergency management. These news services provide what is known as Webcasting. These include:

- After Dark Online (http://www.afterdark.com) mainly news

- BackWeb (http://www.backweb.com) updates in background while you work

- FreeLoader (http://www.freeloader.com) users your browser to download what you preselect

- Castanet (http://www.marimba.com) this system is free and multi-media friendly

- PointCast Network (http://www.pointcast.com) picks up data from a variety of sites

All of these services can be useful can all be useful, just like CNN Interactive, but they slow down many older systems. They have been known to lock up and crash less robust systems (e.g., a 486 with 8 megabytes of RAM). However, if you have anything with Pentium speed, and at least 16 megabytes of RAM, these updating services can run in the background seamlessly and provide that instant access to breaking events critical to emergency management.

Advances in Connectivity

There was a time, not long ago, when a cell phone cost over $1,000 and electronic bulletin boards were for the computer elite. In 1990, I was laughed at during a conversation in California when I predicted that within a year or two I could be sitting in my car in a parking lot, doing business with anyone in the world; that I could be sending faxes and mail to anyone else with a similar capability or a phone system; that I could be printing out other people's documents in the car, editing them, and faxing them back; and, that I could be taking pictures and sending them instantly through the computer to a client. They called me a dreamer in 1991. In 1997, thousands of road warriors do these operations as part of their daily work routines. They are electronically interconnected so the work comes to them.

In 1994 I wrote a paper called "Telecommuting and the Virtual EOC" for a conference in Israel. What I prophesied then is now coming to pass in emergency management. Buildings are becoming more expensive, while transmission of data is becoming more efficient, cheaper and more mobile. Teleworkers are learning the new paradigms of remote operations, including the use of the Internet, to transmit all types of information. There is no reason for the emergency operations center to be static any longer, and the Internet will help make that possible. The Internet will also make response coordination efforts less dependent on buildings that may collapse, loose essential services, or be inaccessible to those who need to staff them. By the end of this century, some larger organizations may have virtual emergency operations centers at a Web Sites where the players will report remotely and work with a virtual picture of each other as they coordinate the resources and decisionmaking needed for disasters. Of course, this will not replace the need for the responders in the field, but it will change how the first responders can access the EOC function. Most of this is already technically feasible. It will be the integration process that takes time. There are two major tools that will make this change more attractive.

White Boarding

The single most underutilized tool in emergency management is white boarding over the Internet. Why emergency managers have not flocked to this concept is puzzling. Is there a single emergency management conference or staff meeting that does not call for at least one grease board with erasable markers? That is how the business has worked for a decade. Grease boards replaced the chalk boards, and are now an essential tool. A white board is nothing more than a grease board on your computer screen. By connecting through the Internet (or your organization's LAN and Intranet) you can work immediate ideas out without ever touching paper. White boarding can incorporate text, graphics, video and audio transmissions. There are a number of vendors available to provide this tool. The authors have no specific preference but we believe Intel will be the leader in this arena, along with IBM.

What does this mean for the emergency manager? Shorter staff meetings, certainly. But during response, there can be critical times when multiple disciplines need to consider operations such as evacuation. With GIS map capability, the white board can be an immediate working tool for making decisions in coordination with field staff. That's just one example. Public Information Officers can work on an instantaneous edit with the key decisionmaker. Logistics staff can present several options on purchases, based on cost, availability and quality. A variety of personnel can give direct input and compare quickly prior to a timely approval. The possibilities are endless. If you take nothing else from this chapter, do yourself a favor and start investing some time with white boarding.

Internet Phones/ CUSeeMe

The second critical tool is audio/visual contact. One of the common beliefs of established emergency managers is that the business will always require eye-to-eye discussions to operate. In the world of Generation Z, and most of Y, that is true. But not the X'ers. No, they have a completely different attitude. Emergency managers need to begin the process of integrating how the next generation will coordinate before, during, and after disasters. That is critical for an effective 21st Century capability.

 The use of telephone communications transmissions is not new. It was one of the earliest proposed capabilities of the Internet. However, the cost of the digital signal process (**DSP**) was so high that only specialized user applications for security and military functions could afford it. Now, anyone can transmit and receive reasonable quality voice transmission over a PC, after minimal investments in hardware and in software applications. Once installed to your existing ISP, your staff can call other locations with the same worldwide capacities at no cost other than those charges your ISP demands for access time. Quality, low-cost, voice transmission is a critical step in virtual Emergency Operation Center capacity. The technology is available. The leading developers are those who also feature audio/visual combinations over the Internet.

Just 5 years ago, transmission of the simplest video over the Internet was a technical nightmare. As of 1997, anyone can transmit black and white video, with voice, for under $100. Color is available for under $400. Those prices include all the software and hardware! All of this is being pushed by the gigantic surge in Internet use. What does this mean for your emergency management strategies? First, if you have multiple field offices, you can now hold real-time video conferences  between all of them without a single cost in travel expenses, or lost time in transit. And the long distance charges for phone calls are gone (unless the FCC gets pushed into charging for such calls in the future). Just the savings from one video conference using the Internet could pay for almost all of the hardware and software upgrades. And, now you have a redundant communications backbone.

This technology can also be used in coordination with EOC operations. If you need to coordinate a video conference with other key EOC section chiefs, you can do so, even if they are in remote locations. The cameras for the systems are so small and light they can be carried in a fanny pack with ease.

This technology by no means provides television quality, and the rate of broadcasting (frames per second) is still slow, but improving. The size of the picture on the screen is also still fairly small. As band width improves (the size of the pipeline for moving data), television quality transmissions will be possible. This is the answer to the face-to-face requirements of some managers. If you shop for one of these products, make sure it complies with the current desktop videoconferencing (**DVC**) standards (e.g., H.323 is the standard in 1997, but H.324 is close behind). The standard ensures your other software will cooperate cleanly with the videoconferencing tool and will produce the best picture available through the Internet. There are many manufacturers to choose from in the videoconferencing world. The authors recommend you focus on one of the following:

- White Pine Software (CUSeeMe)

- VocalTec (Internet phone with video)

- Intel (Internet Video Phone)

- Microsoft (NetMeeting)

- Connectix (VideoPhone)

- VDOnet (VDOPhone)

Communications: Is That All There Is?

Every emergency manager knows that the heart and soul of the business is communications. Outmoded, antiquated systems sometimes create more problems than they solve. Sometimes, however, they are more reliable than the innovations. The last ten years have produced many changes in emergency systems, e.g., the switch to an 800 MHz radio system; the full installation of 9-1-1 emergency lines, with 3-1-1 now backing them up in some communities; and the Emergency Broadcasting System becoming the Emergency Alert System. There is even a ruling from the FCC (E-911) that requires cellular phone companies to be able to locate their clients' signal within 125 meters by the year 2001. Emergency management professionals should watch these changes carefully, or they will find themselves lost in the dust, wondering about the herd that ran over them. It is the same with the Internet. There are some basic concepts in configurations of operations, transmission types, and styles of hardware that you should be familiar with so that, if nothing else, you ask questions of the Information Management Specialist in your organization.

Internet Access, Anytime, Anywhere

When structuring your computer network system for emergency response, it might be wise to interlink it to the Internet, so that whenever a remote worker is hooked to your intranet, he or she is also hooked to the Internet. This can be achieved through a number of software solutions such as those from Microsoft (Remote Access Service) or Novell (NetWare Connect). Or, you may choose to use a hardware solution by installing a stand-alone remote node server. These are offered by several vendors, including Shiva and Cisco. A third option is remote-control software that allows a distant PC to operate a terminal as if the user was at that station. Such software allows a laptop or notebook to connect back to a dummy server. The authors recommend such products as ReachOut (produced by Stac), or pcAnywhere (produced by Symantec).

Before you completely depend on your current ISP, be sure you know the range of access before a call becomes long distance, or if there are restrictions on your connections within a certain geographic range. This is not a problem you want to discover during a disaster. If your ISP has limited range, you may have to go to a national provider, like America Online™ or Prodigy™. There are many such vendors available. They ensure that there is a system capable of being called from anywhere in the US, but the availability of access at any given time of day may be difficult.

If you really want total remote capabilities for access to the Internet, and the virtual EOC, you should consider wireless support from a specialized Internet Service Provider. Until recently, these services were very selective about where they could serve clients. Just like the cellular phone providers, they had specific geographic ranges (usually those with the highest concentration of users). That is improving dramatically. By the end of 1998, there should be almost no location in the continental U.S. that cannot be connected by cellular phone to a wireless ISP. Some of the vendors that are currently major providers are RAM Mobile Data and ARDIS. But also be aware of the competition for line access in the cellular world. By the year 2001 there may be as many as 62 million cell phone users in the US, and almost half of them are expected to be using remote capabilities through their PCs.

One final consideration is what you will do with your total portability. If you want to just use e-mail and text transfers, most wireless services and software will be adequate. However, to take full advantage of the World Wide Web, you need graphics capacity. That is a challenge to wireless systems. Recent answers are being provided through a coalition of vendors of what is called "spread spectrum" technology. They can help solve this problem. You may wish to contact:

- Metricom

- US Robotics (AllPoints modem)

- Wynd Communications

- Go America

- RadioMail

- DTS Wireless

- Locus One

Speed and Volume

As with water, there are two considerations for moving data: how much can flow through the channel, and how fast? The emerging technologies for Internet access are focused directly at these challenges. The new rule of thumb is, "What used to go by wire now goes by air. What used to go through the air will now be carried by a wire." If you grasp that, then you can see the future.

Satellite

Some people have invested in small satellite television during the past few years, mainly with RCA and DirecTV, or Primestar "minidish" systems. The company that offers DirecTV also offers a DirecPC system. This setup consists of an elliptical dish, cable, and an adapter card for your PC system. It offers a speed of up to 400 kilobytes per second incoming to the computer. As with other evolving forms of connectivity, the outgoing speed is much lower than the incoming speed. This may seem like a reasonable alternative, but consider the cost: a  suggested price of $699 for the system, an activation fee of $49.95, and then, monthly fees that range from $24.95 to $129.95, with *NO* option for unlimited use at any given time. Depending on time of day and plan, you can be charged 60 or 80 cents per megabyte above and beyond the limits of your plan. The monthly fees alone can easily be double that of current Internet Service Provider costs. The intent of the DirecPC system is to compete with current Integrated Services Digital Network (**ISDN**) capabilities and costs. However, the satellite system may have a short lifetime with the development of more standardized methods of high-speed telephone system service access, offering comparable, if not superior, speed and cost.

ADSL

Omitting the postal system, the most common and familiar form of communication is the telephone. Many of you use modems or have encountered them at some point during your computer experience. You may have also encountered the speed, or lack thereof, when using such devices through phone lines. When the telephone was created, the inventors determined that the human voice could be transmitted clearly at approximately 3000 hertz. Although we are still using basically the same copper wire, this wire can conduct a range well above and beyond that required to make voices traverse the world. Asymmetric Digital Subscriber Line (**ADSL**) will attempt to bridge this gap and revolutionize telecommunications. Some of you may have had the misfortune of picking up a phone while the modem was in action. The reason you hear all sorts of strange sounds stems from the usage of the 3000 hertz range, but instead of a voice, the modem simply creates and detects subtle changes in sound.

Modems today can achieve speeds of 28.8, 33.6, or even 56.0 kilobits per second. Keep in mind that 8 bits make up a byte, so 56 kilobits is actually 7 kilobytes. Some of you may be familiar with ISDN, which generally provides 64 or 128 kilobits per second. Now what would you say to speeds at least 100 times that of the fastest modem or 40 times that of the fastest standard ISDN line? Say hello to ADSL.

Now, as with many of the fast upcoming alternatives for Internet access, the transfer rate to your computer with ADSL is much greater than the outgoing rate. The minimum testing line speeds right now are 1.5-2.0 megabits per second in and 16 kilobits per second out, which is still a drastic improvement over the standard rate using phone lines. Other locations offer speeds of 6.0 megabits per second in and 64 kilobits per second out. Projections indicate possible speeds of 9.0 megabits per second in and 640 kilobits per second out. That is nearly equivalent to being directly networked on a local area network for incoming data. This is referred to as Very-high bit rate Digital Subcriber Line (**VDSL**) service.

After all of these images of grandeur, you may want to know what, when, where, and how much. Several companies are offering ADSL in select regions, with GTE actually entering a real-world testing phase. The biggest roadblock in this process involves the telephone companies upgrading their switching centers to handle the new technology. Prospects look good, and Pacific Bell estimates nearly half of their customers will be able to utilize ADSL by the end of 1997. Pacific Bell plans to begin public testing in San Francisco during September, 1997. Until your local phone service offers ADSL, the methods of accessing this technology are both difficult and demanding. As for the cost of this service, that will depend on the phone companies and hardware vendors. ADSL devices may not be available for general purchase until 1998. However, as Rate Adaptive Digital Subscriber Line (RADSL) service becomes available, the costs for operating the systems should decrease.

Cable Modems

Millions of people own televisions and millions of people enjoy the crisp, clear, and varied viewing available by cable. In the past year or so, a development in connectivity took advantage of this broad networking: the cable modem. This device allows home users to connect their computers to the cable network. In actuality, the television signal uses only a small fraction of the entire bandwidth of standard cable lines. Separating these signals eliminates the need to keep switching between television transmission and phone line carriers for the Internet signal. Since most EOCs have a television set for monitoring the media, this may be of great advantage to emergency management.

Cable modem access is not available everywhere. However, access has been expanding across the nation quite rapidly. The cable modem adapter can be rented from the cable company at a rate that remains highly competitive with Internet Service Providers and other forms of high-speed home access. The rate can typically range from $15-40 per month. The cable modem adapter provides a standard ethernet interface for your computer; the cost of an ethernet adapter ranges between $50-$100. This makes cable modems a very attractive option for any Internet user and for an EOC that must be designed under a tight budget.

Yes, the cost and the simplicity of using a cable modem make it a good choice for many, but how about performance? Well, this can vary greatly, depending on the number and kinds of connections the cable provider has, and how many other people are using their cable modems at the same time. Generally, available bandwidth varies between 500 kilobytes per second and 2 megabytes per second, but that is no assurance of actual performance. Because of this congestion, many information specialists believe that having both ADSL available for desktop PCs and a cable modem connection as a backup provides a strong, reasonably priced redundancy for access to the Internet.

Fiber Optics

The central structure of the Internet is based on fiber optic connectivity. The current advancement is **ATM** (Asynchronous Transfer Mode) technology. Previous limitations of T1 and T3 line technology now stand aside to the massive capabilities of ATM. The newest and fastest line ratings are mainly two types: OC-3 and OC-12. OC-3 lines can handle 155 megabits per second of information. Many schools and large Internet providers have converted to this speed of line and ATM technology. OC-12 lines provide a whopping 622 megabits per second of information. These are now becoming the very core of the Internet, with such companies as MCI using these for their central data transmission and routing.

If you have fiber optic connectivity, congratulations. Use it to its fullest potential. This was an innovation (although an expensive one) from the late 1970's. However, if you are considering connectivity solutions now, the new ADSL and cable modem options are much more affordable and begin to rival the speeds of the early fiber optics networks. Fiber optics will continue to provide a backbone for the Internet, but not a practical solution for most smaller networking requirements.

Graphics, GIS, GPS

There are three other value-added technologies that are converging to make your Internet connectivity incredibly flexible. Most emergency managers have already adopted the use of computer graphics for their planning, procedures, drills and response operations. These tools have become significant during the push for increased mitigation activities after large losses to natural disasters. One of the truly powerful advances is the portability of not only digital cameras (**DC**), but digital video camcorders (**DVC**).

There are many DCs that can take dozens of high-quality pictures and transfer them directly to a PC. Some DCs hook directly to laptops with wireless capabilities. This allows very fast transmission of graphics for manipulation back at the office or to an EOC. These visual records are easier to store than film, more durable, and easier to share with a large stakeholder base via e-mail.

The DVCs are even more amazing. A video camera that would have cost $10,000 or more in 1990, and cut a hole in your shoulder from carrying it, is now palm size and costs under $3000. Current electronic technologies are advancing in capability at a rate of thirty percent a year. Imagine going to an incident scene and sending back completely edited tape, with special effects, that using the 1 pound DVC unit in your hands. Another value is that most of the DVCs also take digital stills, so there is no need to buy a digital camera, for most emergency management needs, if you have a digital camcorder. That is an immense capability for first responders and emergency managers. The DVCs are available right now and will become as much a part of the emergency manager's tools as the cell phone is today.

The same brand names you have trusted over the years for your 35mm cameras and camcorders are also the leaders in these technologies, such as:

- JVC

- Panasonic

- Sharp

- Canon

Geographic Information Systems (**GIS**) have proven themselves in government service for over twenty years, but it has not been until the last five years that they have proved invaluable to the emergency manager during all phases of operation. The Internet is going to be the biggest source of cross-fertilization as GIS uses increase. More and more World Wide Web Sites are providing GIS files for use by those interested in a jurisdiction's specific details. Many of the popular emergency management softwares (EIS™ and Softrisk™) are adapting to this environment and now include both Internet and GIS applications capacity. The blend of the large file transfer capacity, and the interface of large public access databases, will be even more critical as populations increase. GIS is already a crucial tool for risk management. If your organization has not taken full advantage of GIS technology, and its connection to the Internet, we recommend that you have your Information Management Specialist provide a demonstration for your management as soon as possible.

The added abilities of global positioning systems (**GPS**) is bringing GIS into new focus for emergency managers. A GPS unit uses military satellites to establish the location of individuals within 300 feet of their actual coordinates anywhere on earth. Many U.S. cities now track fire, law and medical vehicles thorough GPS signals. Search-and-Rescue Units use the system to track their teams. Even some wildland parks require hikers to rent a unit before going into especially challenging terrain.

It is expected that these units will increase in use, and drop in price. The authors speculate that the next big application will be for identification of the location of civilians with disabilities, so they can be easily located inside of a disaster zone. The authors also met someone developing a unit that could be attached to children so they could be tracked if abducted. These applications would be tied to the GPS satellites and the cellular phone systems.

There are almost unlimited possibilities for the use of GPS. With the data available from the scene, an EOC director could literally pull up a GIS map through the Internet (or the agency network) and track all of the law, fire, and medical units on scene, as well as the position of the first responders wearing GPS transponders. The map would refresh frequently so the resource logistics could be assessed remotely, beyond the heat of battle. The power of this technology during a terrorist event is immeasurable.

New Concepts of Web Use

There are a few new emergency management concepts that will be highlighted as major breakthroughs in the next few years, and these all have a strong relationship with the Internet.

Internets vs. Intranets

The reach of the Internet is not infinite. It does have some limits on its size and capacity. This may come as a hindrance early in the 21st Century. Many organizations believe that the only countermeasure is to develop an internal network, referred to as an intranet. The best emergency management use of the Internet with an intranet is through gates that can be opened and closed as needed for disasters. For instance, you may have a public Web Site that you want restricted by either access codes or a firewall during emergencies, but which is open during normal operations. You may also want to coordinate databases and GIS functions with some other related organizations through an independent Web Site. The independent site would sample data from both organizations' intranets and load them to a common file so both organizations would have access without penetrating each other's systems. There are lots of options available with this new mix. Work with your Information Management Specialist to find out if there is already an intranet in place in your organization, or if one is being planned.

Voice Commands

The computer technology is not quite at the point yet where an emergency manager can walk to a console and command a computer to go through a series of activities, especially if a number of these are unrelated, without keyboard or mouse manipulations. I stress *yet* because that day is close at hand. This may seem incredible, but the demands of the community with disabilities, increased needs for voice to print capabilities in business, and the need for robot voice commands have spurred this market. There is a time coming in the very near future when staff can walk into an EOC and activate all the power, lights, computer systems and peripherals by voice command.

This technology is already available. IBM has had a software package for several years that turns simple English speech directly into text. This may also one day assist in keeping more accurate, on-the-fly logs during disasters (which are so important for legal and financial reasons after the dust settles). In a future scenario, staff will be able to talk to the PC and ask it to find things on the Internet, without the inconvenience of looking up URL codes, or searching through lists to find an appropriate title. This capacity is likely to be available before the end of this century.

Rapid Assessment Field Teams

A long-awaited process is being developed in emergency management, based on painful lessons learned during the last ten years of mega-loss disasters. The EOC needs better eyes in the field, as soon as possible, to evaluate what is happening at ground zero, and act as an overhead management team to get a broader picture of anticipated resource requirements. Several states have begun to implement this process. The state of Florida has already developed a Rapid Incident Assessment Team (**RIAT**) and the federal government has designated similar teams as part of the Emergency Support Functions (**ESF**). The federal government refers to these as Field Assessment Teams (**FAsT**). What does this have to do with the Internet?

Along with the development of these teams has come another convergent technology that blends computers with field operations. Wearable computers are now in use throughout the world. Their main function has been for military and industrial applications. Now any individual can have access to unlimited stores of technical data and advice by wearing a side-pack unit portable computer, with wireless capacity. A headphone set, and an eyepiece or visor, provides all the audio and visual information. The units often have GPS installed in the packs, as well as full faxing capability. With direct ties to the Internet, LANs, and WANs, there is no limit to the interchange of information. Some units also feature a video camera mount on the headpiece so that a viewer at the EOC could see the same views as the wearer. These units are tough. The military and heavy industry have demanded hardened systems. This is perfect for disaster environments.

If you are interested in wearable computer technologies, consider contacting some of the following vendors:

- Xybernaut Corporation, http://www.xybernaut.com

- ViA Inc., http://www.flexipc.com

- Computing Devices International, http://www.cdev.com

- Phoenix Group, Inc., http://www.ivpgi.com

- Speech Systems Inc., http://www.speechsys.com

- Rockwell International Corporation, http://www.cacd.rockwell.com

Masters Degree in Emergency Management

Imagine finding a remote learning tool that will provide the opportunity for you or your employees to get that next degree, with very little actual attendance at an actual campus. Hard to believe? It's available right now through the Center for the Study of Emergency Management, in association with Hope International University. The extensive course offerings, and the opportunities for independent studies, may make this the best training dollar in the 21st Century. To take advantage of it now, go to their Web Site at: http://www.simeon.org/msm.html

And Last, for the Way, Way Out

For the emergency manager who wants to truly go beyond the cutting edge, to what Californians call the "bleeding edge," the authors have frequented what might be called "fringe technology" Web Sites. Beware, the ideas may leave you struggling for your technological breath. Why? When techno-wizards begin talking about cybergenetics, and combining the computer and the Internet into a person's biology...well, it's not light reading. This is the Extropian movement.

To explore Extropian Principles, visit the following site:
http://www.aleph.se:80/Trans/Cultural/Philosophy/princip.html

To understand the terminology used by the Extropians, visit the following site:
http://www.aleph.se:80/Trans/Words/index.html

The 21st Century may find us in a nanotechnology wonderland where we are no longer outside the Internet, but living within it. We did warn you!

Bright Ideas: Take your Internet Service Provider to lunch today.
Ask the specialist to help you with:

✓ improving the speed/quality of current communications hardware;

✓ updating Internet browsers and assisting with integration of their use; and

✓ installing white boarding software along with integration training for staff.

Acronyms

ABAG	Association of Bay Area Governments
ADSL	Asymmetric Digital Subscriber Line
ALERT	Automated Local Evaluation in Real Time
APWA	American Public Works Association
ARIA	American Risk and Insurance Association
ARRL	American Radio Relay League
ATC	Applied Technology Council
ATM	Asynchronous Transfer Mode
BATF	Bureau of Alcohol, Tobacco and Firearms
BBS	Bulletin Board Service
BGS	British Geological Survey
BNAC	Bureau of National Affairs Communications
BRMA	Business Recovery Manager's Association
CAIC	Colorado Avalanche Information Center
CAN	Community Alert Network
CARICOM	Caribbean Community
CBO	Community Based Organization
CCEP	Canadian Centre for Emergency Preparedness
CD	Compact Disk
CDC	U.S. Center for Disease Control
CDERA	Caribbean Disaster Emergency Response Agency
CEPPO	Chemical Emergency Preparedness and Prevention Office
CERES	California Environmental Resources Evaluation System
CERT	Computer Emergency Response Teams
CERTS	Computer Emergency Response Team Coordination Center
CFR	Code of Federal Regulations
CHAMP	Coastal Hazards Assessment and Mitigation Project
CIA	Central Intelligence Agency
CIC	Consumer Information Center
COE	Center of Excellence
CPMR	Crisis Prevention, Mitigation and Recovery in Africa
CPU	Central Processing Unit
CSTI	California Specialized Training Institute

DC	Digital Camera
DOS	Disk Operating System
DOT	U.S. Department of Transportation
DRIE	Disaster Recovery Information Exchange
DSP	Digital Signal Processor
DVC	Desktop Videoconferencing
DVC	Digital Video Camcorder
E-mail	Electronic Mail
EAS	Emergency Alert System
EERC	Earthquake Engineering Research Center
EERI	Earthquake Engineering Research Institute
EMI	Emergency Management Institute
EMWIN	Emergency Managers Weather Information System
EOC	Emergency Operations Center
EOFIND	Earth Observation for Identification of Natural Disasters
EPA	U.S. Environmental Protection Agency
EPIX	Emergency Preparedness Information Exchange
EQNET	Earthquake Hazards Mitigation Information Network
ERRI	Emergency Response and Research Institute
ESF	Emergency Support Function
FAA	Federal Aviation Administration
FAsT	Field Assessment Team
FAX	Facsimile
FBI	Federal Bureau of Investigation
FCC	Federal Communications Commission
FEAT	Franchise Emergency Action Team
FEMA	Federal Emergency Management Agency
FERC	Federal Energy Regulatory Commission
FHWA	U.S. Federal Highway Administration
FRA	Federal Railroad Administration
GAO	U.S. Government Accounting Office
GCMD	Global Change Master Directory
GEMS	Global Emergency Management Service
GERC	Global Earthquake Response Center
GHCC	Global Hydrology and Climate Center
GILS	Government Information Locator Service
GIS	Geographic Information System
GPS	Global Positioning System
GSRG	Global Seismology Research Group
H.323	A standard for DVC
HMIX	Hazardous Material Information Exchange
HTML	Hypertext Markup Language
IAVCEI	International Association of Volcanology and Chemistry of the Earth's Interior
IAWF	International Association of Wildland Fire

ICBO	International Conference of Building Officials
ICMA	International City/County Management Association
ICRC	International Committee of the Red Cross
IDNDR	International Decade for Natural Disaster Reduction
IIPLR	Insurance Institute for Property Loss Reduction
INCEDE	International Center for Disaster Mitigation Engineering
IPPNW	International Physicians for the Prevention of Nuclear War
IRC	Internet Relay Chat
ISDN	Integrated Services Digital Network
ISP	Internet Service Provider
kbs	Thousand Bytes per Second
LAN	Local Area Network
LRC	Learning Resource Center
MARS	Military Affiliate Radio System
Mbps	Megabits per second
MHz	Megahertz
MMDS	Multi-channel Multi-point Distribution Service
Modem	Modulate-Demodulate
NACEC	North American Center for Emergency Communications
NASA	National Aeronautics and Space Administration
NAVCEN	Navigation Center
NCAR	National Center for Atmospheric Research
NCCEM	National Coordinating Council on Emergency Management
NCEER	National Center for Earthquake Engineering Research
NCTCOG	North Central Texas Council of Governments
NDMC	National Drought Mitigation Center
NEI	Nuclear Energy Institute
NEMA	National Emergency Management Association
NERIN	National Emergency Resource Information Network
NESDIS	National Environmental Satellite, Data and Information Service
NFPA	National Fire Protection Academy
NGDC	National Geophysical Data Center
NHRC	Natural Hazards Research Centre
NI/USR	National Institute of Urban Search and Rescue
NIH	National Institute of Health
NISEE	National Information Service for Earthquake Engineering
NLC	National League of Cities
NLSI	National Lightning Safety Institute
NOAA	National Oceanic and Atmospheric Administration
NRC	Nuclear Regulatory Commission
NSA	National Sheriff's Association
NSSL	National Severe Storms Laboratory
NSTC	National Science and Technology Council
NTSB	National Transportation Safety Board

NUWC	Naval Undersea Warfare Center
NVOAD	National Voluntary Organizations Active in Disaster
NWS	National Weather Service
OES	Office of Emergency Services
PAHO	Pan American Health Organization
PC	Personal Computer
PCDPPP	Pan Caribbean Disaster Preparedness and Prevention Project
RADSL	Rate Adaptive Digital Subscriber Line
RAM	Random Access Memory
RIAT	Rapid Incident Assessment Team
RIMS	Response Information Management System
ROM	Read Only Memory
SALEMDUG	State and Local Emergency Management Data Users Group
SAR	Search and Rescue
SCEC	Southern California Earthquake Center
SNDR	Subcommittee on Natural Disaster Reduction
SOLE	International Society of Logistics
SRA	Society for Risk Analysis
STEND	System for Technology Exchange for Natural Disasters
UNDHA	United Nations Department of Humanitarian Affairs
URL	Uniform Resource Locator
USAR	Urban Search and Rescue
USGS	U.S. Geological Survey
VDSL	Very-high bit rate Digital Subscriber Line
VGA	Variable Graphics Array
VITA	Volunteers in Technical Assistance
WAN	Wide Area Network
WAN	Wide Area Network
WDM	Wavelength Division Multiplexing
WHIMS	Wildfire Hazard Information and Mitigation System
WHO	World Health Organization
WLTF	Wind Load Test Facility
WSSPC	Western States Seismic Policy Council
WWW	World Wide Web

References

Basic Computer Understanding

How Computers Work, Ron White, 1993, Ziff-Davis Press

Inside the Personal Computer, Sharon Gallagher, 1984, Abbeville Press, Inc.

Emergency Management References

Safety and Health on the Internet, Ralph B. Stuart,III, 1997, Government Institutes, Inc.

Environmental Guide to the Internet, Carol Briggs-Erickson and Toni Murphy, 1996, Government Institutes, Inc.

Chemical Guide to the Internet, C.C. Lee, 1996, Government Institutes, Inc.

Emergency Planning and Management, William H. Stringfield, 1996, Government Institutes, Inc.

Disaster Assistance: A Guide to Recovery Programs, FEMA 229(4), November 1995

Disaster Cost Recovery Guidelines: Recovering Costs for Building Damage or Loss and Seeking Payment for Increased Services, Alameda County Card Project, 1996

Microcomputers in Emergency Management: Implementation of Computer Technology, Thomas E. Drabek, Monograph No. 51, Institute of Behavioral Science, University of Colorado, 1991.

Internet Basics

Learning the Internet, Arntson/Berkemeyer/Halliwell.Neuburger, 1997, DDC Publishing

Work Place Dynamics

Transitions, W. Bridges, Don Mills, Workingham, 1980, Addison-Wesley Publishing

Index

0 - 9

A

B

O

V

W

X

Y

Z

GOVERNMENT INSTITUTES ORDER FORM

4 Research Place, Suite 200 • Rockville, MD 20850-3226 • Tel (301) 921-2355 • Fax (301) 921-0373
Internet: *http://www.govinst.com* • E-mail: *giinfo@govinst.com*

3 EASY WAYS TO ORDER

Phone: **(301) 921-2355**
Have your credit card ready when you call.

Fax: **(301) 921-0373**
Fax this completed order form with your company
purchase order or credit card information.

Mail: **Government Institutes**
4 Research Place, Suite 200
Rockville, MD 20850-3226
USA
Mail this completed order form with a check, company
purchase order, or credit card information.

PAYMENT OPTIONS

❏ **Check** (*payable to Government Institutes in US dollars*)

❏ **Purchase Order** (this order form must be attached to your
company P.O. <u>Note</u>: All International orders must be pre-paid.)

❏ **Credit Card** ❏ ❏ ❏

Exp.___/____

Credit Card No. _____

Signature _____
Government Institutes' Federal I.D.# is 52-0994196

CUSTOMER INFORMATION

Ship To: (Please attach your Purchase Order)

Name: _____

GI Account# (*7 digits on mailing label*): _____

Company/Institution: _____

Address: _____
(*please supply street address for UPS shipping*)
_____

City: _____ State/Province: _____

Zip/Postal Code: _____ Country: _____

Tel: ( ) _____

Fax: ( ) _____

E-mail Address: _____

Bill To: (if different than ship to address)

Name: _____

Title/Position: _____

Company/Institution: _____

Address: _____
(*please supply street address for UPS shipping*)
_____

City: _____ State/Province: _____

Zip/Postal Code: _____ Country: _____

Tel: ( ) _____

Fax: ( ) _____

E-mail Address: _____

Qty.	Product Code	Title	Price

New Edition No Obligation Standing Order Program

...ase enroll me in this program for the products I have ordered. Government
...itutes will notify me of new editions by sending me an invoice. I understand
... there is no obligation to purchase the product. This invoice is simply my
...inder that a new edition has been released.

15 DAY MONEY-BACK GUARANTEE

...you're not completely satisfied with any product, return it undamaged
...hin 15 days for a full and immediate refund on the price of the product.

Subtotal_____
MD Residents add 5% Sales Tax_____
Shipping and Handling (see box below)_____
Total Payment Enclosed_____

Within U.S:	**Outside U.S:**
1-4 products: $6/product	Add $15 for each item (Airmail)
5 or more: $3/product	Add $10 for each item (Surface)

SOURCE CODE: BP01

GOVERNMENT INSTITUTES
MINI-CATALOG

PC #	ENVIRONMENTAL TITLES	Pub Date	Price
585	Book of Lists for Regulated Hazardous Substances, 8th Edition	1997	$79
4088	CFR Chemical Lists on CD ROM, 1997 Edition	1997	$125
4089	Chemical Data for Workplace Sampling & Analysis, Single User	1997	$125
512	Clean Water Handbook, 2nd Edition	1996	$89
581	EH&S Auditing Made Easy	1997	$79
587	E H & S CFR Training Requirements, 3rd Edition	1997	$89
4082	EMMI-Envl Monitoring Methods Index for Windows-Network	1997	$537
4082	EMMI-Envl Monitoring Methods Index for Windows-Single User	1997	$179
525	Environmental Audits, 7th Edition	1996	$79
548	Environmental Engineering and Science: An Introduction	1997	$79
578	Environmental Guide to the Internet, 3rd Edition	1997	$59
560	Environmental Law Handbook, 14th Edition	1997	$79
353	Environmental Regulatory Glossary, 6th Edition	1993	$79
562	Environmental Statutes, 1997 Edition	1997	$69
562	Environmental Statutes Book/Disk Package, 1997 Edition	1997	$204
4060	Environmental Statutes on Disk for Windows-Network	1997	$405
4060	Environmental Statutes on Disk for Windows-Single User	1997	$135
570	Environmentalism at the Crossroads	1995	$39
536	ESAs Made Easy	1996	$59
515	Industrial Environmental Management: A Practical Approa ch	1996	$79
4078	IRIS Database-Network	1997	$1,485
4078	IRIS Database-Single User	1997	$495
510	ISO 14000: Understanding Environmental Standards	1996	$69
551	ISO 14001: An Executive Repoert	1996	$55
518	Lead Regulation Handbook	1996	$79
478	Principles of EH&S Management	1995	$69
554	Property Rights: Understanding Government Takings	1997	$79
582	Recycling & Waste Mgmt Guide to the Internet	1997	$49
594	Texas Environmental Regulations Manual	1997	$125
566	TSCA Handbook, 3rd Edition	1997	$95
534	Wetland Mitigation: Mitigation Banking and Other Strategies	1997	$75

PC #	SAFETY AND HEALTH TITLES	Pub Date	Price
547	Construction Safety Handbook	1996	$79
553	Cumulative Trauma Disorders	1997	$59
559	Forklift Safety	1997	$65
539	Fundamentals of Occupational Safety & Health	1996	$49
535	Making Sense of OSHA Compliance	1997	$59
563	Managing Change for Safety and Health Professionals	1997	$59
589	Managing Fatigue in Transportation, *ATA Conference*	1997	$75
4086	OSHA Technical Manual, Electronic Edition	1997	$99
598	Project Mgmt for E H & S Professionals	1997	$59
552	Safety & Health in Agriculture, Forestry and Fisheries	1997	$125
523	Safety & Health on the Internet	1996	$39
597	Safety Is A People Business	1997	$49
463	Safety Made Easy	1995	$49
590	Your Company Safety and Health Manual	1997	$79

Electronic Product available on CD-ROM or Floppy Disk

GOVERNMENT INSTITUTES

PUBLICATIONS CATALOG
1997

PLEASE CALL OUR PUBLISHING DEPARTMENT AT
(301) 921-2355 FOR A FREE PUBLICATIONS CATALOG.

Government Institutes
4 Research Place, Suite 200 • Rockville, MD 20850-3226
Tel. (301) 921-2355 • FAX (301) 921-0373
E mail: giinfo@govinst.com • Internet: http://www.govinst.com